M000032651

Presented to:

_____

By:

_____

GOD'S PROMISES®

— & —

ANSWERS

FOR MEN

A Division of Thomas Nelson
Nashville

Contents

GOD'S PROMISES FOR MEN

GOD'S PLAN FOR MEN IS . . .

To Worship God 2

To Obey God's Word 5

To Come to God in Prayer 8

To Listen to the Holy Spirit 11

GOD FREELY GIVES TO MEN . . .

Eternal Hope for Life 18

Wisdom for Each Day 23

Victory Over Sin 28

Peace in Troubled Times 34

Power to Defeat Their Deepest Fears 38

Courage to Be Men of Integrity 42

GOD ASKS A MAN TO . . .

Witness to the Lost 48

Love His Neighbor 52

Reach Out to the Poor and Homeless 56

Contents

Trust God 61

Honor and Support His Church and Pastor 65

GOD GIVES A MAN STRENGTH WHEN . . .

He Comforts His Loved Ones 70

He Feels Defeated and Powerless 74

A Member of His Family Dies 80

He Is Angry and Needs Peace 84

His Loved Ones Grow Apart 87

GOD CHALLENGES A MAN TO . . .

Grow in His Christian Walk 92

Deal Honestly with Others 96

Ask Forgiveness of Others 99

Share His Faith with Others 101

Be Wise with His Finances 104

Be Accountable to Christian Brothers 107

GOD LISTENS TO A MAN'S PRAYER WHEN . . .

No One Else Will Listen 112

He Asks for Patience 115

He Asks for Guidance from the Holy Spirit . . . 118

He Confesses His Sins and Seeks Forgiveness . . 122

Contents

The Responsibilities of Life Overwhelm Him   125

GOD FILLS A MAN WITH JOY WHEN . . .

He Praises the Lord 130

His Children Grow to Love God 135

He Worships God 137

GOD KEEPS A MAN SECURE WHEN . . .

He Puts God First in His Life 142

He Makes a Major Job Change 145

Worry and Doubt Threaten His Well-Being ... 149

He Doesn't Have Money to Pay the Bills 153

GOD COMFORTS A MAN WHEN . . .

He Feels Inadequate for His Responsibilities ... 158

His Loved Ones Are Ill 161

His Loved Ones Don't Understand Him 164

He Must Discipline His Loved Ones 166

He Feels Powerless to Shield His Loved
Ones from Evil 169

GOD'S LOVE IS WITH A MAN WHEN . . .

He Brings His Problems to God 174

He Relies on God to Guide His Life 181

He Shares His Good Fortune with Others 185

He Prays with His Family 188

He Forgives Those Who Have Offended Him . . 191

GOD REJOICES WHEN A MAN . . .

Anticipates Christ's Return 196

Dedicates His Life to God 200

Trusts and Waits for God's Answers 203

Is Reconciled with His Brother 206

GOD'S ANSWERS FOR MEN

BEGINNING IN CHRIST

How to Know You Are Born Again 212

How to Know the Sufficiency of Jesus 215

What the Blood of Jesus Is to You 218

How to Know the Power of God's Word 221

What the Holy Spirit Is to You 224

How to Abide in Christ 227

How to Build Your Faith 230

Contents

GROWING IN CHRIST

How to Overcome the Carnal Mind 234

How to Overcome Satan 237

How to Recognize Evil 240

How to Overcome Worldliness 243

How to Deal with Lust 246

How to Overcome Pride 249

How to Control Your Tongue 252

How to Be Christ-Centered 255

Understanding the Liberty that Is in Christ . . . 258

How to Praise the Lord 261

How to Have the Joy of the Lord 265

MATURING IN CHRIST

How to Handle Spiritual Trials 270

How to Face Serious Illness 273

How to Handle Suffering 276

How to Survive Financial Problems 280

How to Handle Stress 283

How to Overcome Despair 287

How to Maintain Hope 290

How to Enter Into God's Rest 293

Contents

How to Be Established in Trust 295

How to Face Old Age 298

How to Have God's Divine Protection 302

How to Find Contentment 305

MINISTERING IN CHRIST

What Is True Service? 310

How to Have an Effective Prayer Life 313

How to Be an Effective Witness 317

How to Handle Condemnation 320

Understanding the Leading of the Lord 323

How to Wait on God 326

The Importance of Obedience 330

Giving to God's Work 333

HOPING IN CHRIST

How to Commit Your Life to Christ 338

How to Draw Near to God 341

How to Recover Spiritually 344

How to Obtain God's Promises 347

Contents

UNDERSTANDING IN CHRIST

Understanding the Personality of God 352

How to Receive Understanding 355

Understanding the Fear of the Lord 358

Understanding the Sovereignty of God 361

How to Grasp Eternity 365

UNITING IN CHRIST

The Fellowship of All Believers 370

The Hope for Revival 374

The Signs of the End 377

GOD'S PLAN
FOR MEN IS ...

God's Plan for Men Is . . .
To Worship God

And you shall remember the LORD your God, for it is He who gives you power to get wealth, that He may establish His covenant which He swore to your fathers, as it is this day. Then it shall be, if you by any means forget the LORD your God, and follow other gods, and serve them and worship them, I testify against you this day that you shall surely perish.

DEUTERONOMY 8:18–19

God is Spirit, and those who worship Him must worship in spirit and truth.

JOHN 4:24

The LORD is great and greatly to be praised;
 He is to be feared above all gods.
 Give to the LORD the glory due His name;
 Bring an offering, and come into His courts.
 Oh, worship the LORD in the beauty of
  holiness!
 Tremble before Him, all the earth.

PSALM 96:4, 8–9

For the LORD is the great God,
And the great King above all gods.
In His hand are the deep places of the earth;
The heights of the hills are His also.
The sea is His, for He made it;
And His hands formed the dry land.
Oh come, let us worship and bow down;
Let us kneel before the LORD our Maker.
For He is our God,
And we are the people of His pasture,
And the sheep of His hand.

PSALM 95:3–7

The world is passing away, and the lust of it; but he who does the will of God abides forever.

1 JOHN 2:17

Fear God and give glory to Him, for the hour of His judgment has come; and worship Him who made heaven and earth, the sea and springs of water.

REVELATION 14:7

Finally, my brethren, rejoice in the Lord.

We are the circumcision, who worship God in the Spirit, rejoice in Christ Jesus, and have no confidence in the flesh.

PHILIPPIANS 3:1A, 3

Looking unto Jesus, the author and finisher of our faith, who for the joy that was set before Him endured the cross, despising the shame, and has sat down at the right hand of the throne of God.

For consider Him who endured such hostility from sinners against Himself, lest you become weary and discouraged in your souls.

HEBREWS 12:2–3

Now I, John, saw and heard these things. And when I heard and saw, I fell down to worship before the feet of the angel who showed me these things.

Then he said to me, "See that you do not do that. For I am your fellow servant, and of your brethren the prophets, and of those who keep the words of this book. Worship God."

REVELATION 22:8–9

Exalt the LORD our God,
And worship at His footstool—
He is holy.

Exalt the LORD our God,
And worship at His holy hill;
For the LORD our God is holy.

PSALM 99:5, 9

God's Plan for Men Is . . .
To Obey God's Word

From there you will seek the LORD your God, and you will find Him if you seek Him with all your heart and with all your soul. When you are in distress, and all these things come upon you in the latter days, when you turn to the LORD your God and obey His voice (for the LORD your God is a merciful God), He will not forsake you nor destroy you, nor forget the covenant of your fathers which He swore to them.

DEUTERONOMY 4:29–31

Jesus answered him, saying, "It is written, 'Man shall not live by bread alone, but by every word of God.'"

LUKE 4:4

As for God, His way is perfect;
The word of the LORD is proven;
He is a shield to all who trust in Him.

PSALM 18:30

As newborn babes, desire the pure milk of the word, that you may grow thereby.

1 PETER 2:2

Oh, that they had such a heart in them that they would fear Me and always keep all My commandments, that it might be well with them and with their children forever!

DEUTERONOMY 5:29

Whatever things were written before were written for our learning, that we through the patience and comfort of the Scriptures might have hope.

ROMANS 15:4

The word of God is living and powerful, and sharper than any two-edged sword, piercing even to the division of soul and spirit, and of joints and marrow, and is a discerner of the thoughts and intents of the heart.

HEBREWS 4:12

The law of the LORD is perfect, converting
    the soul;
The testimony of the LORD is sure, making
    wise the simple;
The statutes of the LORD are right,
    rejoicing the heart;
The commandment of the LORD is pure,
    enlightening the eyes.

PSALM 19:7–8

I understand more than the ancients,
Because I keep Your precepts.
I have restrained my feet from every evil way,
That I may keep Your word.

PSALM 119:100–101

You shall observe My judgments and keep My ordinances, to walk in them: I am the LORD your God.

LEVITICUS 18:4

Draw near to God and He will draw near to you. Cleanse your hands, you sinners; and purify your hearts, you double-minded.

JAMES 4:8

As for God, His way is perfect;
The word of the LORD is proven;
He is a shield to all who trust in Him.

PSALM 18:30

Ask, and it will be given to you; seek, and you will find; knock, and it will be opened to you. For everyone who asks receives, and he who seeks finds, and to him who knocks it will be opened.

MATTHEW 7:7–8

Be anxious for nothing, but in everything by prayer and supplication, with thanksgiving, let your requests be made known to God; and the peace of God, which surpasses all understanding, will guard your hearts and minds through Christ Jesus.

PHILIPPIANS 4:6–7

And whatever things you ask in prayer, believing, you will receive.

MATTHEW 21:22

Rejoice always, pray without ceasing, in everything give thanks; for this is the will of God in Christ Jesus for you.

1 THESSALONIANS 5:16–18

If My people who are called by My name will humble themselves, and pray and seek My face, and turn from their wicked ways, then I will hear from heaven, and will forgive their sin and heal their land.

2 CHRONICLES 7:14

Again I say to you that if two of you agree on earth concerning anything that they ask, it will be done for them by My Father in heaven.

MATTHEW 18:19

Praying always with all prayer and supplication in the Spirit, being watchful to this end with all perseverance and supplication for all the saints.

EPHESIANS 6:18

> For the eyes of the LORD are on the
> righteous,
> And His ears are open to their prayers;
> But the face of the LORD is against
> those who do evil.

1 PETER 3:12

Hear a just cause, O LORD,
Attend to my cry;
Give ear to my prayer which is not from
    deceitful lips.

PSALM 17:1

Hear me when I call, O God of my
    righteousness!
You have relieved me in my distress;
Have mercy on me, and hear my prayer.

PSALM 4:1

As His divine power has given to us all things that
pertain to life and godliness, through the knowledge
of Him who called us by glory and virtue, by which
have been given to us exceedingly great and precious
promises, that through these you may be partakers of
the divine nature, having escaped the corruption that
is in the world through lust.

2 PETER 1:3–4

> But those who wait on the LORD
> Shall renew their strength;
> They shall mount up with wings like eagles,
> They shall run and not be weary,
> They shall walk and not faint.

ISAIAH 40:31

But the fruit of the Spirit is love, joy, peace, longsuffering, kindness, goodness, faithfulness, gentleness,
self-control. Against such there is no law. And those
who are Christ's have crucified the flesh with its passions and desires. If we live in the Spirit, let us also
walk in the Spirit.

GALATIANS 5:22–25

Your ears shall hear a word behind you, saying,
"This is the way, walk in it,"
Whenever you turn to the right hand
Or whenever you turn to the left.

ISAIAH 30:21

If you ask anything in My name, I will do it.

If you love Me, keep My commandments. And I will pray the Father, and He will give you another Helper, that He may abide with you forever—the Spirit of truth, whom the world cannot receive, because it neither sees Him nor knows Him; but you know Him, for He dwells with you and will be in you. I will not leave you orphans; I will come to you.

But the Helper, the Holy Spirit, whom the Father will send in My name, He will teach you all things, and bring to your remembrance all things that I said to you.

JOHN 14:14, 15–18, 26

Nevertheless I tell you the truth. It is to your advantage that I go away; for if I do not go away, the Helper will not come to you; but if I depart, I will send Him to you.

However, when He, the Spirit of truth, has come, He will guide you into all truth; for He will not speak on His own authority, but whatever He hears He will speak; and He will tell you things to come.

JOHN 16:7, 13

If the Spirit of Him who raised Jesus from the dead dwells in you, He who raised Christ from the dead will also give life to your mortal bodies through His Spirit who dwells in you.

The Spirit Himself bears witness with our spirit that we are children of God, and if children, then heirs—heirs of God and joint heirs with Christ, if indeed we suffer with Him, that we may also be glorified together.

For I consider that the sufferings of this present time are not worthy to be compared with the glory which shall be revealed in us.

Likewise the Spirit also helps in our weaknesses. For we do not know what we should pray for as we ought, but the Spirit Himself makes intercession for us with groanings which cannot be uttered. Now He who searches the hearts knows what the mind of the Spirit is, because He makes intercession for the saints according to the will of God.

ROMANS 8:11, 16–18, 26–27

Being assembled together with them, He commanded them not to depart from Jerusalem, but to wait for the Promise of the Father, "which," He said, "you have heard from Me; for John truly baptized with water, but you shall be baptized with the Holy Spirit not many days from now."

"But you shall receive power when the Holy Spirit has come upon you; and you shall be witnesses to Me in Jerusalem, and in all Judea and Samaria, and to the end of the earth."

ACTS 1:4–5, 8

For everyone who asks receives, and he who seeks finds, and to him who knocks it will be opened. If a son asks for bread from any father among you, will he give him a stone? Or if he asks for a fish, will he give him a serpent instead of a fish? Or if he asks for an egg, will he offer him a scorpion? If you then, being evil, know how to give good gifts to your children, how much more will your heavenly Father give the Holy Spirit to those who ask Him!

LUKE 11:10–13

For it is God who works in you both to will and to do for His good pleasure.

PHILIPPIANS 2:13

Eye has not seen, nor ear heard,
Nor have entered into the heart of man
The things which God has prepared for
      those who love Him.

But God has revealed them to us through His Spirit. For the Spirit searches all things, yes, the deep things of God. For what man knows the things of a man except the spirit of the man which is in him? Even so no one knows the things of God except the Spirit of God. Now we have received, not the spirit of the world, but the Spirit who is from God, that we might know the things that have been freely given to us by God. These things we also speak, not in words which man's wisdom teaches but which the Holy Spirit teaches, comparing spiritual things with spiritual. But the natural man does not receive the things of the Spirit of God, for they are foolishness to him; nor can he know them, because they are spiritually discerned.

1 CORINTHIANS 2 :9–14

Who also made us sufficient as ministers of the new covenant, not of the letter but of the Spirit; for the letter kills, but the Spirit gives life.

Now the Lord is the Spirit; and where the Spirit of the Lord is, there is liberty. But we all, with unveiled face, beholding as in a mirror the glory of the Lord, are being transformed into the same image from glory to glory, just as by the Spirit of the Lord.

2 CORINTHIANS 3:6, 17–18

GOD FREELY
GIVES TO MEN . . .

Sing to the LORD with thanksgiving;
Sing praises on the harp to our God,
Who covers the heavens with clouds,
Who prepares rain for the earth,
Who makes grass to grow on the mountains.
He gives to the beast its food,
And to the young ravens that cry.
He does not delight in the strength of the
    horse;
He takes no pleasure in the legs of a man.
The LORD takes pleasure in those who fear
    Him,
In those who hope in His mercy.
Praise the LORD, O Jerusalem!
Praise your God, O Zion!
For He has strengthened the bars of your gates;
He has blessed your children within you.

PSALM 147:7–13

But let us who are of the day be sober, putting on the breastplate of faith and love, and as a helmet the hope of salvation. For God did not appoint us to wrath, but to obtain salvation through our Lord Jesus Christ, who died for us, that whether we wake or sleep, we should live together with Him.

Therefore comfort each other and edify one another, just as you also are doing.

1 THESSALONIANS 5:8–11

But God, who is rich in mercy, because of His great love with which He loved us, even when we were dead in trespasses, made us alive together with Christ (by grace you have been saved), and raised us up together, and made us sit together in the heavenly places in Christ Jesus, that in the ages to come He might show the exceeding riches of His grace in His kindness toward us in Christ Jesus.

EPHESIANS 2:4–7

If then you were raised with Christ, seek those things which are above, where Christ is, sitting at the right hand of God. Set your mind on things above, not on things on the earth.

COLOSSIANS 3:1–2

I have been crucified with Christ; it is no longer I who live, but Christ lives in me; and the life which I now live in the flesh I live by faith in the Son of God, who loved me and gave Himself for me.

GALATIANS 2:20

For as many as are led by the Spirit of God, these are sons of God. For you did not receive the spirit of bondage again to fear, but you received the Spirit of adoption by whom we cry out, "Abba, Father." The Spirit Himself bears witness with our spirit that we are children of God, and if children, then heirs— heirs of God and joint heirs with Christ, if indeed we suffer with Him, that we may also be glorified together.

For I consider that the sufferings of this present time are not worthy to be compared with the glory which shall be revealed in us.

For we were saved in this hope, but hope that is seen is not hope; for why does one still hope for what he sees? But if we hope for what we do not see, we eagerly wait for it with perseverance.

ROMANS 8:14–18, 24–25

I have fought the good fight, I have finished the race, I have kept the faith. Finally, there is laid up for me the crown of righteousness, which the Lord, the righteous Judge, will give to me on that Day, and not to me only but also to all who have loved His appearing.

2 TIMOTHY 4:7–8

Blessed be the God and Father of our Lord Jesus Christ, who according to His abundant mercy has begotten us again to a living hope through the resurrection of Jesus Christ from the dead, to an inheritance incorruptible and undefiled and that does not fade away, reserved in heaven for you, who are kept by the power of God through faith for salvation ready to be revealed in the last time.

In this you greatly rejoice, though now for a little while, if need be, you have been grieved by various trials, that the genuineness of your faith, being much more precious than gold that perishes, though it is tested by fire, may be found to praise, honor, and glory at the revelation of Jesus Christ, whom having not seen you love. Though now you do not see Him, yet believing, you rejoice with joy inexpressible and full of glory, receiving the end of your faith—the salvation of your souls.

1 PETER 1:3–9

Because of the hope which is laid up for you in heaven, of which you heard before in the word of the truth of the gospel, which has come to you, as it has also in all the world, and is bringing forth fruit, as it is also among you since the day you heard and knew the grace of God in truth.

COLOSSIANS 1:5–6

My son, pay attention to my wisdom;
Lend your ear to my understanding,
That you may preserve discretion,
And your lips may keep knowledge.

PROVERBS 5:1–2

The fear of the LORD is the beginning of
    wisdom;
A good understanding have all those who do
    His commandments.
His praise endures forever.

PSALM 111:10

The days of our lives are seventy years;
And if by reason of strength they are eighty
    years,
Yet their boast is only labor and sorrow;
For it is soon cut off, and we fly away.
Who knows the power of Your anger?
For as the fear of You, so is Your wrath.
So teach us to number our days,
That we may gain a heart of wisdom.

PSALM 90:10–12

How much better to get wisdom than gold!
And to get understanding is to be chosen
     rather than silver.

PROVERBS 16:16

Get wisdom! Get understanding!
Do not forget, nor turn away from the words
     of my mouth.
Do not forsake her, and she will preserve
     you;
Love her, and she will keep you.
Wisdom is the principal thing;
Therefore get wisdom.
And in all your getting, get understanding.
Exalt her, and she will promote you;
She will bring you honor, when you embrace
     her.
She will place on your head an ornament of
     grace;
A crown of glory she will deliver to you.
Hear, my son, and receive my sayings,
And the years of your life will be many.
I have taught you in the way of wisdom;
I have led you in right paths.

PROVERBS 4:5–11

However, we speak wisdom among those who are mature, yet not the wisdom of this age, nor of the rulers of this age, who are coming to nothing. But we speak the wisdom of God in a mystery, the hidden wisdom which God ordained before the ages for our glory, which none of the rulers of this age knew; for had they known, they would not have crucified the Lord of glory.

1 Corinthians 2:6–8

My son, keep my words,
And treasure my commands within you.
Keep my commands and live,
And my law as the apple of your eye.
Bind them on your fingers;
Write them on the tablet of your heart.
Say to wisdom, "You are my sister,"
And call understanding your nearest kin,
That they may keep you from the immoral
   woman,
From the seductress who flatters with her
   words.

Proverbs 7:1–5

Happy is the man who finds wisdom,
And the man who gains understanding;
For her proceeds are better than the profits of
    silver,
And her gain than fine gold.
She is more precious than rubies,
And all the things you may desire cannot
    compare with her.
Length of days is in her right hand,
In her left hand riches and honor.
Her ways are ways of pleasantness,
And all her paths are peace.
She is a tree of life to those who take hold of
    her,
And happy are all who retain her.
The LORD by wisdom founded the earth;
By understanding He established the heavens;
By His knowledge the depths were broken up,
And clouds drop down the dew.
My son, let them not depart from your
    eyes—
Keep sound wisdom and discretion;
So they will be life to your soul
And grace to your neck.

PROVERBS 3:13–22

But the wisdom that is from above is first pure, then peaceable, gentle, willing to yield, full of mercy and good fruits, without partiality and without hypocrisy.

JAMES 3:17

If any of you lacks wisdom, let him ask of God, who gives to all liberally and without reproach, and it will be given to him. But let him ask in faith, with no doubting, for he who doubts is like a wave of the sea driven and tossed by the wind.

JAMES 1:5–6

The fear of the LORD is the beginning of
    wisdom,
And the knowledge of the Holy One is
    understanding.
If you are wise, you are wise for yourself,
And if you scoff, you will bear it alone.

PROVERBS 9:10, 12

A wise man fears and departs from evil,
But a fool rages and is self-confident.

PROVERBS 14:16

Therefore, if anyone is in Christ, he is a new creation; old things have passed away; behold, all things have become new. Now all things are of God, who has reconciled us to Himself through Jesus Christ, and has given us the ministry of reconciliation, that is, that God was in Christ reconciling the world to Himself, not imputing their trespasses to them, and has committed to us the word of reconciliation.

Now then, we are ambassadors for Christ, as though God were pleading through us: we implore you on Christ's behalf, be reconciled to God. For He made Him who knew no sin to be sin for us, that we might become the righteousness of God in Him.

2 CORINTHIANS 5:17–21

O God, You know my foolishness;
And my sins are not hidden from You.

PSALM 69:5

For as many as are of the works of the law are under the curse; for it is written, "Cursed is everyone who does not continue in all things which are written in the book of the law, to do them." But that no one is justified by the law in the sight of God is evident, for "the just shall live by faith."

GALATIANS 3:10–11

Stand fast therefore in the liberty by which Christ has made us free, and do not be entangled again with a yoke of bondage.

GALATIANS 5:1

And you know that He was manifested to take away our sins, and in Him there is no sin. Whoever abides in Him does not sin. Whoever sins has neither seen Him nor known Him.

Little children, let no one deceive you. He who practices righteousness is righteous, just as He is righteous.

1 JOHN 3:5–7

"Wash yourselves, make yourselves clean;
 Put away the evil of your doings from
      before My eyes.
 Cease to do evil,
 Learn to do good;
 Seek justice,
 Rebuke the oppressor;
 Defend the fatherless,
 Plead for the widow."
"Come now, and let us reason together,"
      Says the LORD,
"Though your sins are like scarlet,
 They shall be as white as snow;
 Though they are red like crimson,
 They shall be as wool.
 If you are willing and obedient,
 You shall eat the good of the land."

ISAIAH 1:16–19

Therefore, since we have this ministry, as we have received mercy, we do not lose heart. But we have renounced the hidden things of shame, not walking in craftiness nor handling the word of God deceitfully, but by manifestation of the truth commending ourselves to every man's conscience in the sight of God. But even if our gospel is veiled, it is veiled to those who are perishing, whose minds the god of this age has blinded, who do not believe, lest the light of the gospel of the glory of Christ, who is the image of God, should shine on them. For we do not preach ourselves, but Christ Jesus the Lord, and ourselves your bondservants for Jesus' sake. For it is the God who commanded light to shine out of darkness, who has shone in our hearts to give the light of the knowledge of the glory of God in the face of Jesus Christ.

2 CORINTHIANS 4:1–6

Finally, my brethren, be strong in the Lord and in the power of His might. Put on the whole armor of God, that you may be able to stand against the wiles of the devil. For we do not wrestle against flesh and blood, but against principalities, against powers, against the rulers of the darkness of this age, against spiritual hosts of wickedness in the heavenly places. Therefore take up the whole armor of God, that you may be able to withstand in the evil day, and having done all, to stand.

Stand therefore, having girded your waist with truth, having put on the breastplate of righteousness, and having shod your feet with the preparation of the gospel of peace; above all, taking the shield of faith with which you will be able to quench all the fiery darts of the wicked one. And take the helmet of salvation, and the sword of the Spirit, which is the word of God; praying always with all prayer and supplication in the Spirit, being watchful to this end with all perseverance and supplication for all the saints.

EPHESIANS 6:10–18

This is the message which we have heard from Him and declare to you, that God is light and in Him is no darkness at all. If we say that we have fellowship with Him, and walk in darkness, we lie and do not practice the truth. But if we walk in the light as He is in the light, we have fellowship with one another, and the blood of Jesus Christ His Son cleanses us from all sin.

If we say that we have no sin, we deceive ourselves, and the truth is not in us. If we confess our sins, He is faithful and just to forgive us our sins and to cleanse us from all unrighteousness. If we say that we have not sinned, we make Him a liar, and His word is not in us.

1 JOHN 1:5–10

O Death, where is your sting?

O Hades, where is your victory?

The sting of death is sin, and the strength of sin is the law. But thanks be to God, who gives us the victory through our Lord Jesus Christ.

Therefore, my beloved brethren, be steadfast, immovable, always abounding in the work of the Lord, knowing that your labor is not in vain in the Lord.

1 CORINTHIANS 15:55–58

For none of us lives to himself, and no one dies to himself.

ROMANS 14:7

> A horse is a vain hope for safety;
> Neither shall it deliver any by its great strength.
> Behold, the eye of the LORD is on those who
>   fear Him,
> On those who hope in His mercy,
> To deliver their soul from death,
> And to keep them alive in famine.
> Our soul waits for the LORD;
> He is our help and our shield.
> For our heart shall rejoice in Him,
> Because we have trusted in His holy name.
> Let Your mercy, O LORD, be upon us,
> Just as we hope in You.

PSALM 33:17–22

> Trust in the LORD with all your heart,
> And lean not on your own understanding;
> In all your ways acknowledge Him,
> And He shall direct your paths.

PROVERBS 3:5–6

Turn Yourself to me, and have mercy on
      me,
For I am desolate and afflicted.
The troubles of my heart have enlarged;
Bring me out of my distresses!
Look on my affliction and my pain,
And forgive all my sins.

PSALM 25:16–18

The LORD builds up Jerusalem;
He gathers together the outcasts of Israel.
He heals the brokenhearted
And binds up their wounds.
Great is our LORD, and mighty in power;
His understanding is infinite.
The LORD lifts up the humble;
He casts the wicked down to the ground.
For He has strengthened the bars of your gates;
He has blessed your children within you.
He makes peace in your borders,
And fills you with the finest wheat.

PSALM 147:2–3, 5–6, 13–14

Peace I leave with you, My peace I give to you; not as
the world gives do I give to you. Let not your heart
be troubled, neither let it be afraid.

JOHN 14:27

Casting all your care upon Him, for He cares for you.

Be sober, be vigilant; because your adversary the devil walks about like a roaring lion, seeking whom he may devour. Resist him, steadfast in the faith, knowing that the same sufferings are experienced by your brotherhood in the world. But may the God of all grace, who called us to His eternal glory by Christ Jesus, after you have suffered a while, perfect, establish, strengthen, and settle you. To Him be the glory and the dominion forever and ever. Amen.

1 PETER 5:7–11

I will be glad and rejoice in Your mercy,
For You have considered my trouble;
You have known my soul in adversities.

PSALM 31:7

I will bless the LORD at all times;
His praise shall continually be in my mouth.
My soul shall make its boast in the LORD;
The humble shall hear of it and be glad.
Oh, magnify the LORD with me,
And let us exalt His name together.
I sought the LORD, and He heard me,
And delivered me from all my fears.
They looked to Him and were radiant,
And their faces were not ashamed.
This poor man cried out, and the LORD
    heard him,
And saved him out of all his troubles.
The angel of the LORD encamps all around
    those who fear Him,
And delivers them.
Oh, taste and see that the LORD is good;
Blessed is the man who trusts in Him!

PSALM 34:1–8

Then Jesus spoke to them again, saying, "I am the light of the world. He who follows Me shall not walk in darkness, but have the light of life."

JOHN 8:12

> I will love You, O LORD, my strength.
> The LORD is my rock and my fortress and
>   my deliverer;
> My God, my strength, in whom I will trust;
> My shield and the horn of my salvation, my
>   stronghold.
> I will call upon the LORD, who is worthy to
>   be praised;
> So shall I be saved from my enemies.

PSALM 18:1–3

The LORD is my light and my salvation;
Whom shall I fear?
The LORD is the strength of my life;
Of whom shall I be afraid?
When the wicked came against me
To eat up my flesh,
My enemies and foes,
They stumbled and fell.
Though an army may encamp against me,
My heart shall not fear;
Though war may rise against me,
In this I will be confident.
One thing I have desired of the LORD,
That will I seek:
That I may dwell in the house of the LORD
All the days of my life,
To behold the beauty of the LORD,
And to inquire in His temple.
For in the time of trouble
He shall hide me in His pavilion;
In the secret place of His tabernacle
He shall hide me;
He shall set me high upon a rock.

PSALM 27:1–5

For You will light my lamp;
The LORD my God will enlighten my
     darkness.
For by You I can run against a troop,
By my God I can leap over a wall.
As for God, His way is perfect;
The word of the LORD is proven;
He is a shield to all who trust in Him.

                  PSALM 18:28–30

Delight yourself also in the LORD,
And He shall give you the desires of your
     heart.
Commit your way to the LORD,
Trust also in Him,
And He shall bring it to pass.
He shall bring forth your righteousness as
     the light,
And your justice as the noonday.

                  PSALM 37:4–6

Do not be afraid of sudden terror,
Nor of trouble from the wicked when it
     comes;
For the LORD will be your confidence,
And will keep your foot from being caught.

                  PROVERBS 3:25–26

Yet in all these things we are more than conquerors through Him who loved us. For I am persuaded that neither death nor life, nor angels nor principalities nor powers, nor things present nor things to come, nor height nor depth, nor any other created thing, shall be able to separate us from the love of God which is in Christ Jesus our Lord.

ROMANS 8:37–39

> The sun shall no longer be your light by day,
> Nor for brightness shall the moon give light
>   to you;
> But the LORD will be to you an everlasting
>   light,
> And your God your glory.
> Your sun shall no longer go down,
> Nor shall your moon withdraw itself;
> For the LORD will be your everlasting light,
> And the days of your mourning shall be
>   ended.

ISAIAH 60:19–20

Blessed is the man
Who walks not in the counsel of the
        ungodly,
Nor stands in the path of sinners,
Nor sits in the seat of the scornful;
But his delight is in the law of the LORD,
And in His law he meditates day and night.
He shall be like a tree
Planted by the rivers of water,
That brings forth its fruit in its season,
Whose leaf also shall not wither;
And whatever he does shall prosper.
The ungodly are not so,
But are like the chaff which the wind drives
        away.
Therefore the ungodly shall not stand in
        the judgment,
Nor sinners in the congregation of the
        righteous.
For the LORD knows the way of the
        righteous,
But the way of the ungodly shall perish.

PSALM 1:1–6

A good man deals graciously and lends;
He will guide his affairs with discretion.
Surely he will never be shaken;
The righteous will be in everlasting
     remembrance.
He will not be afraid of evil tidings;
His heart is steadfast, trusting in the LORD.

                                        PSALM 112:5–7

Blessed are the undefiled in the way,
Who walk in the law of the LORD!
Blessed are those who keep His testimonies,
Who seek Him with the whole heart!
They also do no iniquity;
They walk in His ways.
You have commanded us
To keep Your precepts diligently.
Oh, that my ways were directed
To keep Your statutes!
Then I would not be ashamed,
When I look into all Your commandments.
I will praise You with uprightness of heart,
When I learn Your righteous judgments.
I will keep Your statutes;
Oh, do not forsake me utterly!

                                        PSALM 119:1–8

Dishonest scales are an abomination to the
      LORD,
But a just weight is His delight.
When pride comes, then comes shame;
But with the humble is wisdom.
The integrity of the upright will guide them,
But the perversity of the unfaithful will
      destroy them.

PROVERBS 11:1–3

He who speaks truth declares righteousness,
But a false witness, deceit.
There is one who speaks like the piercings
      of a sword,
But the tongue of the wise promotes health.
The truthful lip shall be established forever,
But a lying tongue is but for a moment.

PROVERBS 12:17–19

The righteous man walks in his integrity;
His children are blessed after him.

PROVERBS 20:7

The LORD shall judge the peoples;
Judge me, O LORD, according to my
      righteousness,
And according to my integrity within me.

PSALM 7:8

Moreover Job continued his discourse, and said:
"As God lives, who has taken away my justice,
And the Almighty, who has made my soul
      bitter,
As long as my breath is in me,
And the breath of God in my nostrils,
My lips will not speak wickedness,
Nor my tongue utter deceit.
Far be it from me
That I should say you are right;
Till I die I will not put away my integrity
        from me.
My righteousness I hold fast, and will not
      let it go;
My heart shall not reproach me as long as
      I live.

JOB 27:1–6

If I have walked with falsehood,
Or if my foot has hastened to deceit,
Let me be weighed on honest scales,
That God may know my integrity.

JOB 31:5–6

GOD ASKS
A MAN TO . . .

— ❧❧ —

Go therefore and make disciples of all the nations, baptizing them in the name of the Father and of the Son and of the Holy Spirit, teaching them to observe all things that I have commanded you; and lo, I am with you always, even to the end of the age. Amen.

MATTHEW 28:19–20

Therefore God also has highly exalted Him and given Him the name which is above every name, that at the name of Jesus every knee should bow, of those in heaven, and of those on earth, and of those under the earth, and that every tongue should confess that Jesus Christ is Lord, to the glory of God the Father.

PHILIPPIANS 2:9–11

Also I say to you, whoever confesses Me before men, him the Son of Man also will confess before the angels of God. But he who denies Me before men will be denied before the angels of God.

LUKE 12:8–9

I say to you that likewise there will be more joy in heaven over one sinner who repents than over ninety-nine just persons who need no repentance.

LUKE 15:7

For the Son of Man has come to seek and to save that which was lost.

LUKE 19:10

The Spirit of the LORD is upon Me,
Because He has anointed Me
To preach the gospel to the poor;
He has sent Me to heal the brokenhearted,
To proclaim liberty to the captives
And recovery of sight to the blind,
To set at liberty those who are oppressed.

LUKE 4:18

Therefore whoever confesses Me before men, him I will also confess before My Father who is in heaven. But whoever denies Me before men, him I will also deny before My Father who is in heaven.

MATTHEW 10:32–33

Behold, I stand at the door and knock. If anyone hears My voice and opens the door, I will come in to him and dine with him, and he with Me.

REVELATION 3:20

He who has the Son has life; he who does not have the Son of God does not have life.

1 JOHN 5:12

Let your light so shine before men, that they may see your good works and glorify your Father in heaven.

MATTHEW 5:16

And He said to them, "Go into all the world and preach the gospel to every creature. He who believes and is baptized will be saved; but he who does not believe will be condemned."

MARK 16:15–16

If anyone serves Me, let him follow Me; and where I am, there My servant will be also. If anyone serves Me, him My Father will honor.

JOHN 12:26

For God so loved the world that He gave His only begotten Son, that whoever believes in Him should not perish but have everlasting life. For God did not send His Son into the world to condemn the world, but that the world through Him might be saved.

JOHN 3:16–17

The Lord is not slack concerning His promise, as some count slackness, but is longsuffering toward us, not willing that any should perish but that all should come to repentance.

2 PETER 3:9

Those who are wise shall shine like the brightness of the firmament, and those who turn many to righteousness like the stars forever and ever.

DANIEL 12:3

But he, wanting to justify himself, said to Jesus, "And who is my neighbor?"

Then Jesus answered and said: "A certain man went down from Jerusalem to Jericho, and fell among thieves, who stripped him of his clothing, wounded him, and departed, leaving him half dead. Now by chance a certain priest came down that road. And when he saw him, he passed by on the other side. Likewise a Levite, when he arrived at the place, came and looked, and passed by on the other side. But a certain Samaritan, as he journeyed, came where he was. And when he saw him, he had compassion. So he went to him and bandaged his wounds, pouring on oil and wine; and he set him on his own animal, brought him to an inn, and took care of him. On the next day, when he departed, he took out two denarii, gave them to the innkeeper, and said to him, 'Take care of him; and whatever more you spend, when I come again, I will repay you.' So which of these three do you think was neighbor to him who fell among the thieves?"

And he said, "He who showed mercy on him."

Then Jesus said to him, "Go and do likewise."

LUKE 10:29–37

You shall love your neighbor as yourself.

MATTHEW 19:19B

You shall not bear false witness against your neighbor.
You shall not covet your neighbor's house; you shall not covet your neighbor's wife, nor his male servant, nor his female servant, nor his ox, nor his donkey, nor anything that is your neighbor's.

EXODUS 20:16–17

He who despises his neighbor sins;
But he who has mercy on the poor,
    happy is he.

PROVERBS 14:21

He who is devoid of wisdom despises his
    neighbor,
But a man of understanding holds his peace.

PROVERBS 11:12

You shall not cheat your neighbor, nor rob him.

LEVITICUS 19:13A

Do not go hastily to court;
For what will you do in the end,
When your neighbor has put you to shame?
Debate your case with your neighbor,
And do not disclose the secret to another.

PROVERBS 25:8–9

And do not be conformed to this world, but be transformed by the renewing of your mind, that you may prove what is that good and acceptable and perfect will of God.

For I say, through the grace given to me, to everyone who is among you, not to think of himself more highly than he ought to think, but to think soberly, as God has dealt to each one a measure of faith.

ROMANS 12:2–3

Whoever secretly slanders his neighbor,
Him I will destroy;
The one who has a haughty look and a proud
      heart,
Him I will not endure.
My eyes shall be on the faithful of the land,
That they may dwell with me;
He who walks in a perfect way,
He shall serve me.
He who works deceit shall not dwell within
      my house;
He who tells lies shall not continue in my
      presence.

PSALM 101:5–7

Do not say to your neighbor,
"Go, and come back,
And tomorrow I will give it,"
When you have it with you.
Do not devise evil against your neighbor,
For he dwells by you for safety's sake.

PROVERBS 3:28–29

Then the King will say to those on His right hand, "Come, you blessed of My Father, inherit the kingdom prepared for you from the foundation of the world: for I was hungry and you gave Me food; I was thirsty and you gave Me drink; I was a stranger and you took Me in; I was naked and you clothed Me; I was sick and you visited Me; I was in prison and you came to Me."

Then the righteous will answer Him, saying, "Lord, when did we see You hungry and feed You, or thirsty and give You drink? When did we see You a stranger and take You in, or naked and clothe You? Or when did we see You sick, or in prison, and come to You?" And the King will answer and say to them, "Assuredly, I say to you, inasmuch as you did it to one of the least of these My brethren, you did it to Me."

MATTHEW 25:34–40

And above all things have fervent love for one another, for love will cover a multitude of sins. Be hospitable to one another without grumbling. As each one has received a gift, minister it to one another, as good stewards of the manifold grace of God.

1 PETER 4:8–10

Is it not to share your bread with the hungry,
And that you bring to your house the poor
      who are cast out;
When you see the naked, that you cover him,
And not hide yourself from your own flesh?
Then your light shall break forth like the
      morning,
Your healing shall spring forth speedily,
And your righteousness shall go before you;
The glory of the LORD shall be your rear
      guard.
Then you shall call, and the LORD will
      answer;
You shall cry, and He will say, "Here I am."
If you take away the yoke from your midst,
The pointing of the finger, and speaking
      wickedness,
If you extend your soul to the hungry
And satisfy the afflicted soul,
Then your light shall dawn in the darkness,
And your darkness shall be as the noonday.
The LORD will guide you continually,
And satisfy your soul in drought,
And strengthen your bones;
You shall be like a watered garden,
And like a spring of water, whose waters do
      not fail.

ISAIAH 58:7–11

Whoever shuts his ears to the cry of the poor
Will also cry himself and not be heard.

PROVERBS 21:13

Let brotherly love continue. Do not forget to enter-
tain strangers, for by so doing some have unwittingly
entertained angels.

HEBREWS 13:1–2

For the needy shall not always be forgotten;
The expectation of the poor shall not perish
      forever.
Arise, O LORD,
Do not let man prevail;
Let the nations be judged in Your sight.

PSALM 9:18–19

When you reap the harvest of your land, you shall not
wholly reap the corners of your field, nor shall you
gather the gleanings of your harvest. And you shall not
glean your vineyard, nor shall you gather every grape of
your vineyard; you shall leave them for the poor and
the stranger: I am the LORD your God.

LEVITICUS 19:9–10

Defend the poor and fatherless;
Do justice to the afflicted and needy.
Deliver the poor and needy;
Free them from the hand of the wicked.

PSALM 82:3–4

Happy is he who has the God of Jacob
    for his help,
Whose hope is in the LORD his God,
Who made heaven and earth,
The sea, and all that is in them;
Who keeps truth forever,
Who executes justice for the oppressed,
Who gives food to the hungry.
The LORD gives freedom to the prisoners.
The LORD opens the eyes of the blind;
The LORD raises those who are bowed down;
The LORD loves the righteous.
The LORD watches over the strangers;
He relieves the fatherless and widow;
But the way of the wicked He turns upside
    down.
The LORD shall reign forever—
Your God, O Zion, to all generations.
Praise the LORD!

PSALM 146:5–10

But whoever has this world's goods, and sees his brother in need, and shuts up his heart from him, how does the love of God abide in him?

My little children, let us not love in word or in tongue, but in deed and in truth. And by this we know that we are of the truth, and shall assure our hearts before Him.

1 JOHN 3:17–19

If a brother or sister is naked and destitute of daily food, and one of you says to them, "Depart in peace, be warmed and filled," but you do not give them the things which are needed for the body, what does it profit? Thus also faith by itself, if it does not have works, is dead.

JAMES 2:15–17

Behold, He who keeps Israel
Shall neither slumber nor sleep.
The LORD is your keeper;
The LORD is your shade at your right hand.
The sun shall not strike you by day,
Nor the moon by night.
The LORD shall preserve you from all evil;
He shall preserve your soul.
The LORD shall preserve your going out
    and your coming in
From this time forth, and even
    forevermore.

PSALM 121:4–8

Oh, the depth of the riches both of the wisdom and knowledge of God! How unsearchable are His judgments and His ways past finding out!

    For who has known the mind of the LORD?
    Or who has become His counselor?
    Or who has first given to Him
    And it shall be repaid to him?
    For of Him and through Him and to Him are all things, to whom be glory forever. Amen.

ROMANS 11:33–36

Then Job answered and said:
"Even today my complaint is bitter;
My hand is listless because of my groaning."

JOB 23:1–2

In the day of my trouble I will call upon You,
For You will answer me.
Among the gods there is none like You, O Lord;
Nor are there any works like Your works.
All nations whom You have made
Shall come and worship before You, O Lord,
And shall glorify Your name.
For You are great, and do wondrous things;
You alone are God.

PSALM 86:7–10

Then they cried out to the LORD in their
        trouble,
And He saved them out of their distresses.
He sent His word and healed them,
And delivered them from their destructions.

PSALM 107:19–20

Trust in the LORD with all your heart,
And lean not on your own understanding;
In all your ways acknowledge Him,
And He shall direct your paths.

PROVERBS 3:5–6

And he said:
"The LORD is my rock and my fortress and
     my deliverer;
The God of my strength, in whom I will trust;
My shield and the horn of my salvation,
My stronghold and my refuge;
My Savior, You save me from violence."

2 SAMUEL 22:2–3

Though He slay me, yet will I trust Him.
Even so, I will defend my own ways before
     Him.
He also shall be my salvation.

JOB 13:15–16A

Preserve me, O God, for in You I put my trust.
O my soul, you have said to the LORD,
"You are my Lord,
My goodness is nothing apart from You."

PSALM 16:1–2

But know that the LORD has set apart for
    Himself him who is godly;
The LORD will hear when I call to Him.
Be angry, and do not sin.
Meditate within your heart on your bed,
    and be still.
Offer the sacrifices of righteousness,
And put your trust in the LORD.

PSALM 4:3–5

And we urge you, brethren, to recognize those who labor among you, and are over you in the Lord and admonish you, and to esteem them very highly in love for their work's sake. Be at peace among yourselves.

1 THESSALONIANS 5:12–13

Remember those who rule over you, who have spoken the word of God to you, whose faith follow, considering the outcome of their conduct.

Obey those who rule over you, and be submissive, for they watch out for your souls, as those who must give account. Let them do so with joy and not with grief, for that would be unprofitable for you.

HEBREWS 13:7, 17

Likewise you younger people, submit yourselves to your elders. Yes, all of you be submissive to one another, and be clothed with humility, for

"God resists the proud,
But gives grace to the humble."

1 PETER 5:5

If we endure,
We shall also reign with Him.
If we deny Him,
He also will deny us.

2 TIMOTHY 2:12

LORD, who may abide in Your tabernacle?
Who may dwell in Your holy hill?
He who walks uprightly,
And works righteousness,
And speaks the truth in his heart.

PSALM 15:1–2

For as the body is one and has many members, but all the members of that one body, being many, are one body, so also is Christ. For by one Spirit we were all baptized into one body—whether Jews or Greeks, whether slaves or free—and have all been made to drink into one Spirit. For in fact the body is not one member but many.

If the foot should say, "Because I am not a hand, I am not of the body," is it therefore not of the body? And if the ear should say, "Because I am not an eye, I am not of the body," is it therefore not of the body? If the whole body were an eye, where would be the hearing? If the whole were hearing, where would be the smelling? But now God has set the members, each one of them, in the body just as He pleased. And if they were all one member, where would the body be?

But now indeed there are many members, yet one body. And the eye cannot say to the hand, "I have no need of you"; nor again the head to the feet, "I have no need of you." No; much rather, those members of the body which seem to be weaker are necessary. And those members of the body which we think to be less honorable, on these we bestow greater honor; and our unpresentable parts have greater modesty, but our presentable parts have no need. But God composed the body, having given greater honor to that part which lacks it, that there should be no schism in the body, but that the members should have the same care for one another. And if one member suffers, all the members suffer with it; or if one member is honored, all the members rejoice with it.

Now you are the body of Christ, and members individually. And God has appointed these in the church: first apostles, second prophets, third teachers, after that miracles, then gifts of healings, helps, administrations, varieties of tongues.

1 CORINTHIANS 12:12–28

You are complete in Him, who is the head of all principality and power.

And not holding fast to the Head, from whom all the body, nourished and knit together by joints and ligaments, grows with the increase that is from God.

COLOSSIANS 2:10–19

For as we have many members in one body, but all the members do not have the same function, so we, being many, are one body in Christ, and individually members of one another.

ROMANS 12:4–5

Behold, how good and how pleasant it is
For brethren to dwell together in unity!

PSALM 133:1

He Himself gave some to be apostles, some prophets, some evangelists, and some pastors and teachers, for the equipping of the saints for the work of ministry, for the edifying of the body of Christ.

EPHESIANS 4:11–12

GOD GIVES A MAN
STRENGTH WHEN . . .

But the mercy of the LORD is from
      everlasting to everlasting
On those who fear Him,
And His righteousness to children's children.

PSALM 103:17

He will feed His flock like a shepherd;
He will gather the lambs with His arm,
And carry them in His bosom,
And gently lead those who are with young.

ISAIAH 40:11

Are not two sparrows sold for a copper coin? And not one of them falls to the ground apart from your Father's will. But the very hairs of your head are all numbered. Do not fear therefore; you are of more value than many sparrows.

MATTHEW 10:29–31

Now we exhort you, brethren, warn those who are unruly, comfort the fainthearted, uphold the weak, be patient with all. See that no one renders evil for evil to anyone, but always pursue what is good both for yourselves and for all.

1 THESSALONIANS 5:14–15

Fear not, for I am with you;
Be not dismayed, for I am your God.
I will strengthen you,
Yes, I will help you,
I will uphold you with My righteous
    right hand.
Behold, I will make you into a new threshing
    sledge with sharp teeth;
You shall thresh the mountains and beat
    them small,
And make the hills like chaff.
You shall winnow them, the wind shall
    carry them away,
And the whirlwind shall scatter them;
You shall rejoice in the LORD,
And glory in the Holy One of Israel.

ISAIAH 41:10, 15–16

Blessed be the God and Father of our Lord Jesus Christ, the Father of mercies and God of all comfort, who comforts us in all our tribulation, that we may be able to comfort those who are in any trouble, with the comfort with which we ourselves are comforted by God. For as the sufferings of Christ abound in us, so our consolation also abounds through Christ.

2 CORINTHIANS 1:3–5

> When the waves of death surrounded me,
> The floods of ungodliness made me afraid.
> The sorrows of Sheol surrounded me;
> The snares of death confronted me.
> In my distress I called upon the LORD,
> And cried out to my God;
> He heard my voice from His temple,
> And my cry entered His ears.

2 SAMUEL 22:5–7

Therefore comfort each other and edify one another, just as you also are doing.

1 THESSALONIANS 5:11

We then who are strong ought to bear with the scruples of the weak, and not to please ourselves. Let each of us please his neighbor for his good, leading to edification. For even Christ did not please Himself; but as it is written, "The reproaches of those who reproached You fell on Me." For whatever things were written before were written for our learning, that we through the patience and comfort of the Scriptures might have hope.

ROMANS 15:1–4

Sing, O heavens!
Be joyful, O earth!
And break out in singing, O mountains!
For the LORD has comforted His people,
And will have mercy on His afflicted.
But Zion said, "The LORD has forsaken me,
And my LORD has forgotten me."
Can a woman forget her nursing child,
And not have compassion on the son of
her womb?
Surely they may forget,
Yet I will not forget you.
See, I have inscribed you on the palms of
My hands;
Your walls are continually before Me.

ISAIAH 49:13–16

God is our refuge and strength,
A very present help in trouble.
Therefore we will not fear,
Even though the earth be removed,
And though the mountains be carried into
    the midst of the sea;
Though its waters roar and be troubled,
Though the mountains shake with its swelling.

PSALM 46:1–3

Trouble and anguish have overtaken me,
Yet Your commandments are my delights.
The righteousness of Your testimonies is
    everlasting;
Give me understanding, and I shall live.

PSALM 119:143–144

And those who know Your name will put
    their trust in You;
For You, LORD, have not forsaken those
    who seek You.

PSALM 9:10

Bow down Your ear, O LORD, hear me;
For I am poor and needy.
Preserve my life, for I am holy;
You are my God;
Save Your servant who trusts in You!
Be merciful to me, O Lord,
For I cry to You all day long.
Rejoice the soul of Your servant,
For to You, O Lord, I lift up my soul.
For You, Lord, are good, and ready to forgive,
And abundant in mercy to all those who
        call upon You.
Give ear, O LORD, to my prayer;
And attend to the voice of my supplications.

PSALM 86:1–6

I cried out to You, O LORD:
I said, "You are my refuge,
My portion in the land of the living.
Attend to my cry,
For I am brought very low;
Deliver me from my persecutors,
For they are stronger than I.
Bring my soul out of prison,
That I may praise Your name;
The righteous shall surround me,
For You shall deal bountifully with me."

PSALM 142:5–7

He who dwells in the secret place of the
      Most High
Shall abide under the shadow of the Almighty.
I will say of the LORD, "He is my refuge
      and my fortress;
My God, in Him I will trust."
Surely He shall deliver you from the snare
      of the fowler
And from the perilous pestilence.
He shall cover you with His feathers,
And under His wings you shall take refuge;
His truth shall be your shield and buckler.
You shall not be afraid of the terror by night,
Nor of the arrow that flies by day,
Nor of the pestilence that walks in darkness,
Nor of the destruction that lays waste at
      noonday.
A thousand may fall at your side,
And ten thousand at your right hand;
But it shall not come near you.
Only with your eyes shall you look,
And see the reward of the wicked.
Because you have made the LORD, who
      is my refuge,
Even the Most High, your dwelling place,
No evil shall befall you,
Nor shall any plague come near your dwelling.

PSALM 91:1–10

Concerning this thing I pleaded with the Lord three times that it might depart from me. And He said to me, "My grace is sufficient for you, for My strength is made perfect in weakness." Therefore most gladly I will rather boast in my infirmities, that the power of Christ may rest upon me. Therefore I take pleasure in infirmities, in reproaches, in needs, in persecutions, in distresses, for Christ's sake. For when I am weak, then I am strong.

2 CORINTHIANS 12:8–10

And I, brethren, when I came to you, did not come with excellence of speech or of wisdom declaring to you the testimony of God. For I determined not to know anything among you except Jesus Christ and Him crucified. I was with you in weakness, in fear, and in much trembling. And my speech and my preaching were not with persuasive words of human wisdom, but in demonstration of the Spirit and of power, that your faith should not be in the wisdom of men but in the power of God.

1 CORINTHIANS 2:1–5

Give ear to my words, O LORD,
Consider my meditation.
Give heed to the voice of my cry,
My King and my God,
For to You I will pray.
My voice You shall hear in the morning,
        O LORD;
In the morning I will direct it to You,
And I will look up.
For You are not a God who takes pleasure in
        wickedness,
Nor shall evil dwell with You.
The boastful shall not stand in Your sight;
You hate all workers of iniquity.
You shall destroy those who speak falsehood;
The LORD abhors the bloodthirsty and
        deceitful man.
But as for me, I will come into Your house
        in the multitude of Your mercy;
In fear of You I will worship toward Your
        holy temple.
Lead me, O LORD, in Your righteousness
        because of my enemies;
Make Your way straight before my face.
But let all those rejoice who put their
        trust in You;

Let them ever shout for joy, because You
    defend them;
Let those also who love Your name
Be joyful in You.
For You, O LORD, will bless the righteous;
With favor You will surround him as with a
    shield.

PSALM 5:1–8, 11–12

He heals the brokenhearted
And binds up their wounds.
He counts the number of the stars;
He calls them all by name.
Great is our Lord, and mighty in power;
His understanding is infinite.

PSALM 147:3–5

But I do not want you to be ignorant, brethren, concerning those who have fallen asleep, lest you sorrow as others who have no hope. For if we believe that Jesus died and rose again, even so God will bring with Him those who sleep in Jesus.

For this we say to you by the word of the Lord, that we who are alive and remain until the coming of the Lord will by no means precede those who are asleep. For the Lord Himself will descend from heaven with a shout, with the voice of an archangel, and with the trumpet of God. And the dead in Christ will rise first.

1 THESSALONIANS 4:13–16

Your kingdom is an everlasting kingdom,
And Your dominion endures throughout all
    generations.
The LORD upholds all who fall,
And raises up all who are bowed down.

PSALM 145:13–14

For if the dead do not rise, then Christ is not risen. And if Christ is not risen, your faith is futile; you are still in your sins! Then also those who have fallen asleep in Christ have perished. If in this life only we have hope in Christ, we are of all men the most pitiable.

But now Christ is risen from the dead, and has become the firstfruits of those who have fallen asleep. For since by man came death, by Man also came the resurrection of the dead. For as in Adam all die, even so in Christ all shall be made alive. But each one in his own order: Christ the firstfruits, afterward those who are Christ's at His coming. Then comes the end, when He delivers the kingdom to God the Father, when He puts an end to all rule and all authority and power. For He must reign till He has put all enemies under His feet. The last enemy that will be destroyed is death.

1 CORINTHIANS 15:16–26

For I am persuaded that neither death nor life, nor angels nor principalities nor powers, nor things present nor things to come, nor height nor depth, nor any other created thing, shall be able to separate us from the love of God which is in Christ Jesus our Lord.

ROMANS 8:38–39

> To everything there is a season,
> A time for every purpose under heaven:
>> A time to be born,
> And a time to die;
>> A time to plant,
> And a time to pluck what is planted;
>> A time to kill,
> And a time to heal;
>> A time to break down,
> And a time to build up;
>> A time to weep,
> And a time to laugh;
>> A time to mourn,
> And a time to dance;
>> A time to cast away stones,
> And a time to gather stones;
>> A time to embrace,
> And a time to refrain from embracing;
>> A time to gain,
> And a time to lose;

A time to keep,
And a time to throw away;
A time to tear,
And a time to sew;
A time to keep silence,
And a time to speak;
A time to love,
And a time to hate;
A time of war,
And a time of peace.

ECCLESIASTES 3:1–8

Behold, how good and how pleasant it is
For brethren to dwell together in unity!
It is like the precious oil upon the head,
Running down on the beard,
The beard of Aaron,
Running down on the edge of his garments.
It is like the dew of Hermon,
Descending upon the mountains of Zion;
For there the LORD commanded the
      blessing—
Life forevermore.

PSALM 133:1–3

He who is slow to wrath has great understanding,
But he who is impulsive exalts folly.

PROVERBS 14:29

Better is a dinner of herbs where love is,
Than a fatted calf with hatred.
A wrathful man stirs up strife,
But he who is slow to anger allays contention.

PROVERBS 15:17–18

So then, my beloved brethren, let every man be swift to hear, slow to speak, slow to wrath; for the wrath of man does not produce the righteousness of God.

JAMES 1:19–20

He who is slow to anger is better than
    the mighty,
And he who rules his spirit than he who
    takes a city.

PROVERBS 16:32

The beginning of strife is like releasing
    water;
Therefore stop contention before a
    quarrel starts.

PROVERBS 17:14

For God is not the author of confusion but of peace, as in all the churches of the saints.

1 CORINTHIANS 14:33

Be angry, and do not sin: do not let the sun go down on your wrath.

EPHESIANS 4:26

Let your speech always be with grace, seasoned with salt, that you may know how you ought to answer each one.

Colossians 4:6

Now I plead with you, brethren, by the name of our Lord Jesus Christ, that you all speak the same thing, and that there be no divisions among you, but that you be perfectly joined together in the same mind and in the same judgment.

1 Corinthians 1:10

Therefore my spirit is overwhelmed within me;
My heart within me is distressed.
I remember the days of old;
I meditate on all Your works;
I muse on the work of Your hands.
I spread out my hands to You;
My soul longs for You like a thirsty land.
Answer me speedily, O LORD;
My spirit fails!
Do not hide Your face from me,
Lest I be like those who go down into the pit.
Cause me to hear Your lovingkindness in
     the morning,
For in You do I trust;
Cause me to know the way in which I
     should walk,
For I lift up my soul to You.

PSALM 143:4–8

He who heeds the word wisely will
     find good,
And whoever trusts in the LORD, happy is he.

PROVERBS 16:20

A merry heart makes a cheerful countenance,
But by sorrow of the heart the spirit is broken.
The heart of him who has understanding
seeks knowledge,
But the mouth of fools feeds on foolishness.
All the days of the afflicted are evil,
But he who is of a merry heart has a
continual feast.
Better is a little with the fear of the LORD,
Than great treasure with trouble.

PROVERBS 15:13–16

But Jesus knew their thoughts, and said to them: "Every kingdom divided against itself is brought to desolation, and every city or house divided against itself will not stand."

MATTHEW 12:25

A brother offended is harder to win than a
strong city,
And contentions are like the bars of a castle.

PROVERBS 18:19

A merry heart does good, like medicine,
But a broken spirit dries the bones.

PROVERBS 17:22

Better is a dry morsel with quietness,
Than a house full of feasting with strife.

PROVERBS 17:1

Pursue peace with all people, and holiness, without which no one will see the Lord: looking carefully lest anyone fall short of the grace of God; lest any root of bitterness springing up cause trouble, and by this many become defiled.

HEBREWS 12:14–15

GOD CHALLENGES
A MAN TO . . .

GOD CHALLENGES A MAN TO . . . GROW IN HIS CHRISTIAN WALK

Teach me, O LORD, the way of Your statutes,
And I shall keep it to the end.
Give me understanding, and I shall keep
    Your law;
Indeed, I shall observe it with my whole heart.
Make me walk in the path of Your
    commandments,
For I delight in it.

PSALM 119:33–35

Now by this we know that we know Him, if we keep His commandments. He who says, "I know Him," and does not keep His commandments, is a liar, and the truth is not in him. But whoever keeps His word, truly the love of God is perfected in him. By this we know that we are in Him. He who says he abides in Him ought himself also to walk just as He walked.

1 JOHN 2:3–6

Therefore, having these promises, beloved, let us cleanse ourselves from all filthiness of the flesh and spirit, perfecting holiness in the fear of God.

2 CORINTHIANS 7:1

God's Promises

Your word is a lamp to my feet
And a light to my path.
I have sworn and confirmed
That I will keep Your righteous judgments.
I am afflicted very much;
Revive me, O LORD, according to Your word.
Accept, I pray, the freewill offerings of my
      mouth, O LORD,
And teach me Your judgments.
My life is continually in my hand,
Yet I do not forget Your law.

PSALM 119:105–109

Apply your heart to instruction,
And your ears to words of knowledge.

PROVERBS 23:12

Teach me Your way, O LORD;
I will walk in Your truth;
Unite my heart to fear Your name.
I will praise You, O Lord my God,
      with all my heart,
And I will glorify Your name forevermore.

PSALM 86:11–12

Fight the good fight of faith, lay hold on eternal life, to which you were also called and have confessed the good confession in the presence of many witnesses.

1 TIMOTHY 6:12

That the righteous requirement of the law might be fulfilled in us who do not walk according to the flesh but according to the Spirit. For those who live according to the flesh set their minds on the things of the flesh, but those who live according to the Spirit, the things of the Spirit. For to be carnally minded is death, but to be spiritually minded is life and peace.

ROMANS 8:4–6

Two men went up to the temple to pray, one a Pharisee and the other a tax collector. The Pharisee stood and prayed thus with himself, "God, I thank You that I am not like other men—extortioners, unjust, adulterers, or even as this tax collector. I fast twice a week; I give tithes of all that I possess." And the tax collector, standing afar off, would not so much as raise his eyes to heaven, but beat his breast, saying, "God, be merciful to me a sinner!" I tell you, this man went down to his house justified rather than the other; for everyone who exalts himself will be humbled, and he who humbles himself will be exalted.

LUKE 18:10–14

And do this, knowing the time, that now it is high time to awake out of sleep; for now our salvation is nearer than when we first believed. The night is far spent, the day is at hand. Therefore let us cast off the works of darkness, and let us put on the armor of light. Let us walk properly, as in the day, not in revelry and drunkenness, not in lewdness and lust, not in strife and envy. But put on the Lord Jesus Christ, and make no provision for the flesh, to fulfill its lusts.

ROMANS 13:11–14

Whoever believes that Jesus is the Christ is born of God, and everyone who loves Him who begot also loves him who is begotten of Him. By this we know that we love the children of God, when we love God and keep His commandments. For this is the love of God, that we keep His commandments. And His commandments are not burdensome.

1 JOHN 5:1–3

Judge not, that you be not judged. For with what judgment you judge, you will be judged; and with the measure you use, it will be measured back to you. And why do you look at the speck in your brother's eye, but do not consider the plank in your own eye? Or how can you say to your brother, "Let me remove the speck from your eye;" and look, a plank is in your own eye? Hypocrite! First remove the plank from your own eye, and then you will see clearly to remove the speck from your brother's eye.

MATTHEW 7:1–5

Do not lie to one another, since you have put off the old man with his deeds, and have put on the new man who is renewed in knowledge according to the image of Him who created him.

COLOSSIANS 3:9–10

Do not withhold good from those to
whom it is due,
When it is in the power of your hand to do so.
PROVERBS 3:27

Lying lips are an abomination to the LORD,
But those who deal truthfully are His delight.
PROVERBS 12:22

Then the LORD sent Nathan to David. And he came
to him, and said to him: "There were two men in one
city, one rich and the other poor. The rich man had
exceedingly many flocks and herds. But the poor man
had nothing, except one little ewe lamb which he had
bought and nourished; and it grew up together with
him and with his children. It ate of his own food and
drank from his own cup and lay in his bosom; and it
was like a daughter to him. And a traveler came to the
rich man, who refused to take from his own flock and
from his own herd to prepare one for the wayfaring
man who had come to him; but he took the poor
man's lamb and prepared it for the man who had
come to him."

So David's anger was greatly aroused against
the man, and he said to Nathan, "As the LORD lives,
the man who has done this shall surely die! And he
shall restore fourfold for the lamb, because he did this
thing and because he had no pity."

Then Nathan said to David, "You are the man!"
2 SAMUEL 12:1–7A

And take not the word of truth utterly
    out of my mouth,
For I have hoped in Your ordinances.
So shall I keep Your law continually,
Forever and ever.
And I will walk at liberty,
For I seek Your precepts.

PSALM 119:43–45

If indeed you have heard Him and have been taught
by Him, as the truth is in Jesus: that you put off, concerning your former conduct, the old man which
grows corrupt according to the deceitful lusts, and be
renewed in the spirit of your mind.

EPHESIANS 4:21–23

A man's pride will bring him low,
But the humble in spirit will retain honor.

PROVERBS 29:23

Take heed to yourselves. If your brother sins against you, rebuke him; and if he repents, forgive him. And if he sins against you seven times in a day, and seven times in a day returns to you, saying, "I repent," you shall forgive him.

LUKE 17:3–4

Whenever you stand praying, if you have anything against anyone, forgive him, that your Father in heaven may also forgive you your trespasses. But if you do not forgive, neither will your Father in heaven forgive your trespasses.

MARK 11:25–26

I, therefore, the prisoner of the Lord, beseech you to walk worthy of the calling with which you were called, with all lowliness and gentleness, with longsuffering, bearing with one another in love, endeavoring to keep the unity of the Spirit in the bond of peace.

EPHESIANS 4:1–3

Bearing with one another, and forgiving one another, if anyone has a complaint against another; even as Christ forgave you, so you also must do.

COLOSSIANS 3:13

For if you forgive men their trespasses, your heavenly Father will also forgive you. But if you do not forgive men their trespasses, neither will your Father forgive your trespasses.

MATTHEW 6:14–15

Let all bitterness, wrath, anger, clamor, and evil speaking be put away from you, with all malice. And be kind to one another, tenderhearted, forgiving one another, even as God in Christ forgave you.

EPHESIANS 4:31–32

He who covers his sins will not prosper,
But whoever confesses and forsakes
them will have mercy.

PROVERBS 28:13

Repay no one evil for evil. Have regard for good things in the sight of all men. If it is possible, as much as depends on you, live peaceably with all men. Beloved, do not avenge yourselves, but rather give place to wrath; for it is written, "Vengeance is Mine, I will repay," says the Lord.

ROMANS 12:17–19

But what does it say? The word is near you, in your mouth and in your heart (that is, the word of faith which we preach): that if you confess with your mouth the Lord Jesus and believe in your heart that God has raised Him from the dead, you will be saved. For with the heart one believes unto righteousness, and with the mouth confession is made unto salvation. For the Scripture says, "Whoever believes on Him will not be put to shame."

ROMANS 10:8–11

For the equipping of the saints for the work of ministry, for the edifying of the body of Christ, till we all come to the unity of the faith and of the knowledge of the Son of God, to a perfect man, to the measure of the stature of the fullness of Christ; that we should no longer be children, tossed to and fro and carried about with every wind of doctrine, by the trickery of men, in the cunning craftiness of deceitful plotting, but, speaking the truth in love, may grow up in all things into Him who is the head—Christ.

EPHESIANS 4:12–15

For this is good and acceptable in the sight of God our Savior, who desires all men to be saved and to come to the knowledge of the truth.

1 TIMOTHY 2:3–4

Brethren, if anyone among you wanders from the truth, and someone turns him back, let him know that he who turns a sinner from the error of his way will save a soul from death and cover a multitude of sins.

JAMES 5:19–20

A woman of Samaria came to draw water. Jesus said to her, "Give Me a drink." For His disciples had gone away into the city to buy food.

JOHN 4:7–8

Most assuredly, I say to you, he who believes in Me, the works that I do he will do also; and greater works than these he will do, because I go to My Father. And whatever you ask in My name, that I will do, that the Father may be glorified in the Son.

JOHN 14:12–13

And let us not grow weary while doing good, for in due season we shall reap if we do not lose heart. Therefore, as we have opportunity, let us do good to all, especially to those who are of the household of faith.

GALATIANS 6:9–10

His lord said to him, "Well done, good and faithful servant; you were faithful over a few things, I will make you ruler over many things. Enter into the joy of your lord."

MATTHEW 25:21

Give, and it will be given to you: good measure, pressed down, shaken together, and running over will be put into your bosom. For with the same measure that you use, it will be measured back to you.

LUKE 6:38

There is one who scatters, yet increases more;
And there is one who withholds more than
is right,
But it leads to poverty.
The generous soul will be made rich,
And he who waters will also be watered himself.

PROVERBS 11:24–25

Those who are wise shall shine
Like the brightness of the firmament,
And those who turn many to righteousness
Like the stars forever and ever.

DANIEL 12:3

Now it shall come to pass, if you diligently obey the voice of the LORD your God, to observe carefully all His commandments which I command you today, that the LORD your God will set you high above all nations of the earth. And all these blessings shall come upon you and overtake you, because you obey the voice of the LORD your God:

Blessed shall you be in the city, and blessed shall you be in the country.

Blessed shall be the fruit of your body, the produce of your ground and the increase of your herds, the increase of your cattle and the offspring of your flocks.

Blessed shall be your basket and your kneading bowl.

Blessed shall you be when you come in, and blessed shall you be when you go out.

DEUTERONOMY 28:1–6

And you shall remember the LORD your God, for it is He who gives you power to get wealth, that He may establish His covenant which He swore to your fathers, as it is this day.

DEUTERONOMY 8:18

Trust in the LORD, and do good;
Dwell in the land, and feed on His faithfulness.
Delight yourself also in the LORD,
And He shall give you the desires of
  your heart.
Commit your way to the LORD,
Trust also in Him,
And He shall bring it to pass.

PSALM 37:3–5

So that you do not appear to men to be fasting, but to your Father who is in the secret place; and your Father who sees in secret will reward you openly.

Do not lay up for yourselves treasures on earth, where moth and rust destroy and where thieves break in and steal; but lay up for yourselves treasures in heaven, where neither moth nor rust destroys and where thieves do not break in and steal. For where your treasure is, there your heart will be also.

MATTHEW 6:18–21

Then you will prosper, if you take care to fulfill the statutes and judgments with which the LORD charged Moses concerning Israel. Be strong and of good courage; do not fear nor be dismayed.

1 CHRONICLES 22:13

The LORD makes poor and makes rich;
He brings low and lifts up.
He raises the poor from the dust
And lifts the beggar from the ash heap,
To set them among princes
And make them inherit the throne of glory.
For the pillars of the earth are the LORD's,
And He has set the world upon them.
He will guard the feet of His saints,
But the wicked shall be silent in darkness.
For by strength no man shall prevail.

1 SAMUEL 2:7–9

"Bring all the tithes into the storehouse,
  That there may be food in My house,
  And try Me now in this,"
Says the LORD of hosts,
"If I will not open for you the windows
        of heaven
  And pour out for you such blessing
  That there will not be room enough to
        receive it."

MALACHI 3:10

Two are better than one,
Because they have a good reward for
    their labor.
For if they fall, one will lift up his
    companion.
But woe to him who is alone when he falls,
For he has no one to help him up.

ECCLESIASTES 4:9–10

Be kindly affectionate to one another with brotherly love, in honor giving preference to one another.

ROMANS 12:10

A man who has friends must himself
    be friendly,
But there is a friend who sticks closer than
    a brother.

PROVERBS 18:24

As iron sharpens iron,
So a man sharpens the countenance of
    his friend.

PROVERBS 27:17

Confess your trespasses to one another, and pray for one another, that you may be healed. The effective, fervent prayer of a righteous man avails much.

JAMES 5:16

And if one member suffers, all the members suffer with it; or if one member is honored, all the members rejoice with it.

1 CORINTHIANS 12:26

For now we see in a mirror, dimly, but then face to face. Now I know in part, but then I shall know just as I also am known.

1 CORINTHIANS 13:12

Abide in Me, and I in you. As the branch cannot bear fruit of itself, unless it abides in the vine, neither can you, unless you abide in Me.

I am the vine, you are the branches. He who abides in Me, and I in him, bears much fruit; for without Me you can do nothing.

JOHN 15:4–5

Since you have purified your souls in obeying the truth through the Spirit in sincere love of the brethren, love one another fervently with a pure heart.

1 PETER 1:22

A new commandment I give to you, that you love one another; as I have loved you, that you also love one another.

JOHN 13:34

I, therefore, the prisoner of the Lord, beseech you to walk worthy of the calling with which you were called, with all lowliness and gentleness, with long-suffering, bearing with one another in love, endeavoring to keep the unity of the Spirit in the bond of peace.

EPHESIANS 4:1–3

Let each of you look out not only for his own interests, but also for the interests of others.

PHILIPPIANS 2:4

Brethren, if anyone among you wanders from the truth, and someone turns him back, let him know that he who turns a sinner from the error of his way will save a soul from death and cover a multitude of sins.

JAMES 5:19–20

Brethren, if a man is overtaken in any trespass, you who are spiritual restore such a one in a spirit of gentleness, considering yourself lest you also be tempted.

GALATIANS 6:1

Finally, all of you be of one mind, having compassion for one another; love as brothers, be tenderhearted, be courteous; not returning evil for evil or reviling for reviling, but on the contrary blessing, knowing that you were called to this, that you may inherit a blessing.

1 PETER 3:8–9

GOD LISTENS TO
A MAN'S PRAYER WHEN

. . .

Ask, and it will be given to you; seek, and you will find; knock, and it will be opened to you. For everyone who asks receives, and he who seeks finds, and to him who knocks it will be opened.

MATTHEW 7:7–8

Continue earnestly in prayer, being vigilant in it with thanksgiving.

COLOSSIANS 4:2

Rejoicing in hope, patient in tribulation, continuing steadfastly in prayer.

ROMANS 12:12

Rejoice always, pray without ceasing, in everything give thanks; for this is the will of God in Christ Jesus for you.

1 THESSALONIANS 5:16–18

If My people who are called by My name will humble themselves, and pray and seek My face, and turn from their wicked ways, then I will hear from heaven, and will forgive their sin and heal their land.

2 CHRONICLES 7:14

Again I say to you that if two of you agree on earth concerning anything that they ask, it will be done for them by My Father in heaven.

MATTHEW 18:19

Hear a just cause, O LORD,
Attend to my cry;
Give ear to my prayer which is not
    from deceitful lips.

PSALM 17:1

Therefore take up the whole armor of God, that you may be able to withstand in the evil day, and having done all, to stand.

Stand therefore, having girded your waist with truth, having put on the breastplate of righteousness, and having shod your feet with the preparation of the gospel of peace; above all, taking the shield of faith with which you will be able to quench all the fiery darts of the wicked one. And take the helmet of salvation, and the sword of the Spirit, which is the word of God; praying always with all prayer and supplication in the Spirit, being watchful to this end with all perseverance and supplication for all the saints.

EPHESIANS 6:13–18

For the eyes of the LORD are on the
    righteous,
And His ears are open to their prayers;
But the face of the LORD is against those
    who do evil.

1 PETER 3:12

Hear me when I call, O God of my
    righteousness!
You have relieved me in my distress;
Have mercy on me, and hear my prayer.

PSALM 4:1

Let us therefore come boldly to the throne of grace,
that we may obtain mercy and find grace to help in
time of need.

HEBREWS 4:16

So I say to you, ask, and it will be given to you; seek,
and you will find; knock, and it will be opened to you.

LUKE 11:9

My brethren, count it all joy when you fall into various trials, knowing that the testing of your faith produces patience. But let patience have its perfect work, that you may be perfect and complete, lacking nothing.

JAMES 1:2–4

And a servant of the Lord must not quarrel but be gentle to all, able to teach, patient.

2 TIMOTHY 2:24

Therefore we also, since we are surrounded by so great a cloud of witnesses, let us lay aside every weight, and the sin which so easily ensnares us, and let us run with endurance the race that is set before us.

HEBREWS 12:1

Now we exhort you, brethren, warn those who are unruly, comfort the fainthearted, uphold the weak, be patient with all.

1 THESSALONIANS 5:14

Therefore if there is any consolation in Christ, if any comfort of love, if any fellowship of the Spirit, if any affection and mercy, fulfill my joy by being like-minded, having the same love, being of one accord, of one mind. Let nothing be done through selfish ambition or conceit, but in lowliness of mind let each esteem others better than himself. Let each of you look out not only for his own interests, but also for the interests of others.

PHILIPPIANS 2:1–4

> But those who wait on the LORD
> Shall renew their strength;
> They shall mount up with wings like eagles,
> They shall run and not be weary,
> They shall walk and not faint.

ISAIAH 40:31

> Wait on the LORD;
> Be of good courage,
> And He shall strengthen your heart;
> Wait, I say, on the LORD!

PSALM 27:14

Rest in the LORD, and wait patiently for
    Him;
Do not fret because of him who prospers in
    his way,
Because of the man who brings wicked
    schemes to pass.
Cease from anger, and forsake wrath;
Do not fret—it only causes harm.
For evildoers shall be cut off;
But those who wait on the LORD,
They shall inherit the earth.

PSALM 37:7–9

The end of a thing is better than its beginning;
The patient in spirit is better than the
    proud in spirit.

ECCLESIASTES 7:8

For even Christ did not please Himself; but as it is
written, "The reproaches of those who reproached
You fell on Me." For whatever things were written
before were written for our learning, that we through
the patience and comfort of the Scriptures might
have hope. Now may the God of patience and comfort grant you to be like-minded toward one another,
according to Christ Jesus.

ROMANS 15:3–5

Teach me to do Your will,
For You are my God;
Your Spirit is good.
Lead me in the land of uprightness.
Revive me, O LORD, for Your name's sake!
For Your righteousness' sake bring my
        soul out of trouble.

PSALM 143:10–11

Now the Lord is the Spirit; and where the Spirit of
the Lord is, there is liberty. But we all, with unveiled
face, beholding as in a mirror the glory of the Lord,
are being transformed into the same image from glory
to glory, just as by the Spirit of the Lord.

2 CORINTHIANS 3:17–18

"He who believes in Me, as the Scripture has said, out
of his heart will flow rivers of living water." But this
He spoke concerning the Spirit, whom those believing in Him would receive; for the Holy Spirit was not
yet given, because Jesus was not yet glorified.

JOHN 7:38–39

I say then: Walk in the Spirit, and you shall not fulfill the lust of the flesh. For the flesh lusts against the Spirit, and the Spirit against the flesh; and these are contrary to one another, so that you do not do the things that you wish. But if you are led by the Spirit, you are not under the law.

Now the works of the flesh are evident, which are: adultery, fornication, uncleanness, lewdness, idolatry, sorcery, hatred, contentions, jealousies, outbursts of wrath, selfish ambitions, dissensions, heresies, envy, murders, drunkenness, revelries, and the like; of which I tell you beforehand, just as I also told you in time past, that those who practice such things will not inherit the kingdom of God.

But the fruit of the Spirit is love, joy, peace, longsuffering, kindness, goodness, faithfulness, gentleness, self-control. Against such there is no law. And those who are Christ's have crucified the flesh with its passions and desires. If we live in the Spirit, let us also walk in the Spirit. Let us not become conceited, provoking one another, envying one another.

GALATIANS 5:16–26

But God has revealed them to us through His Spirit. For the Spirit searches all things, yes, the deep things of God. For what man knows the things of a man except the spirit of the man which is in him? Even so no one knows the things of God except the Spirit of God. Now we have received, not the spirit of the world, but the Spirit who is from God, that we might know the things that have been freely given to us by God.

These things we also speak, not in words which man's wisdom teaches but which the Holy Spirit teaches, comparing spiritual things with spiritual. But the natural man does not receive the things of the Spirit of God, for they are foolishness to him; nor can he know them, because they are spiritually discerned. But he who is spiritual judges all things, yet he himself is rightly judged by no one. For "who has known the mind of the LORD that he may instruct Him?" But we have the mind of Christ.

1 CORINTHIANS 2:10–16

And I will pray the Father, and He will give you another Helper, that He may abide with you forever—the Spirit of truth, whom the world cannot receive, because it neither sees Him nor knows Him; but you know Him, for He dwells with you and will be in you.

JOHN 14:16–17

Nevertheless I tell you the truth. It is to your advantage that I go away; for if I do not go away, the Helper will not come to you; but if I depart, I will send Him to you.

However, when He, the Spirit of truth, has come, He will guide you into all truth; for He will not speak on His own authority, but whatever He hears He will speak; and He will tell you things to come.

JOHN 16:7, 13

By this we know that we abide in Him, and He in us, because He has given us of His Spirit.

1 JOHN 4:13

He who covers his sins will not prosper,
But whoever confesses and forsakes them
    will have mercy.

PROVERBS 28:13

The LORD is far from the wicked,
But He hears the prayer of the righteous.
The light of the eyes rejoices the heart,
And a good report makes the bones healthy.
The ear that hears the rebukes of life
Will abide among the wise.
He who disdains instruction despises his
    own soul,
But he who heeds rebuke gets understanding.
The fear of the LORD is the instruction of
    wisdom,
And before honor is humility.

PROVERBS 15:29–33

If we confess our sins, He is faithful and just to forgive
us our sins and to cleanse us from all unrighteousness.

1 JOHN 1:9

For I will be merciful to their unrighteousness, and their sins and their lawless deeds I will remember no more.

HEBREWS 8:12

Let the wicked forsake his way,
And the unrighteous man his thoughts;
Let him return to the LORD,
And He will have mercy on him;
And to our God,
For He will abundantly pardon.

ISAIAH 55:7

To the praise of the glory of His grace, by which He has made us accepted in the Beloved.

In Him we have redemption through His blood, the forgiveness of sins, according to the riches of His grace.

EPHESIANS 1:6–7

"Come now, and let us reason together,"
Says the LORD,
"Though your sins are like scarlet,
They shall be as white as snow;
Though they are red like crimson,
They shall be as wool."

ISAIAH 1:18

Blessed is he whose transgression is forgiven,
Whose sin is covered.
Blessed is the man to whom the LORD does
      not impute iniquity,
And in whose spirit there is no deceit.

PSALM 32:1–2

My little children, these things I write to you, so that you may not sin. And if anyone sins, we have an Advocate with the Father, Jesus Christ the righteous.

1 JOHN 2:1

"For the mountains shall depart
And the hills be removed,
But My kindness shall not depart from you,
Nor shall My covenant of peace
be removed,"
Says the LORD, who has mercy on you.

ISAIAH 54:10

Be strong and of good courage, do not fear nor be afraid of them; for the LORD your God, He is the One who goes with you. He will not leave you nor forsake you.

DEUTERONOMY 31:6

Therefore, brethren, stand fast and hold the traditions which you were taught, whether by word or our epistle.

Now may our Lord Jesus Christ Himself, and our God and Father, who has loved us and given us everlasting consolation and good hope by grace, comfort your hearts and establish you in every good word and work.

2 THESSALONIANS 2:15–17

For I know the thoughts that I think toward you, says the LORD, thoughts of peace and not of evil, to give you a future and a hope. Then you will call upon Me and go and pray to Me, and I will listen to you. And you will seek Me and find Me, when you search for Me with all your heart.

JEREMIAH 29:11–13

Unless the LORD builds the house,
They labor in vain who build it;
Unless the LORD guards the city,
The watchman stays awake in vain.
It is vain for you to rise up early,
To sit up late,
To eat the bread of sorrows;
For so He gives His beloved sleep.
Behold, children are a heritage from
   the LORD,
The fruit of the womb is a reward.
Like arrows in the hand of a warrior,
So are the children of one's youth.
Happy is the man who has his quiver full
   of them;
They shall not be ashamed,
But shall speak with their enemies in the gate.

PSALM 127:1–5

I cried out to God with my voice—
To God with my voice;
And He gave ear to me.
I remembered God, and was troubled;
I complained, and my spirit was overwhelmed.

PSALM 77:1, 3

Lift up your eyes on high,
And see who has created these things,
Who brings out their host by number;
He calls them all by name,
By the greatness of His might
And the strength of His power;
Not one is missing.
Why do you say, O Jacob,
And speak, O Israel:
"My way is hidden from the LORD,
And my just claim is passed over by my God"?
Have you not known?
Have you not heard?
The everlasting God, the LORD,
The Creator of the ends of the earth,
Neither faints nor is weary.
His understanding is unsearchable.
He gives power to the weak,
And to those who have no might
    He increases strength.

ISAIAH 40:26–29

When you pass through the waters, I will
    be with you;
And through the rivers, they shall not
    overflow you.
When you walk through the fire, you
    shall not be burned,
Nor shall the flame scorch you.
Fear not, for I am with you;
I will bring your descendants from the east,
And gather you from the west;
I will say to the north, "Give them up!"
And to the south, "Do not keep them back!"
Bring My sons from afar,
And My daughters from the ends of
    the earth—
Everyone who is called by My name,
Whom I have created for My glory;
I have formed him, yes, I have made him.

                                    ISAIAH 43:2, 5–7

GOD FILLS A MAN
WITH JOY WHEN . . .

GOD FILLS A MAN WITH JOY WHEN . . .
HE PRAISES THE LORD

I will extol You, my God, O King;
And I will bless Your name forever and ever.
Every day I will bless You,
And I will praise Your name forever and ever.
Great is the LORD, and greatly to be praised;
And His greatness is unsearchable.
One generation shall praise Your works
        to another,
And shall declare Your mighty acts.

PSALM 145:1–4

Both young men and maidens;
Old men and children.
Let them praise the name of the LORD,
For His name alone is exalted;
His glory is above the earth and heaven.
And He has exalted the horn of His people,
The praise of all His saints—
Of the children of Israel,
A people near to Him.
Praise the LORD!

PSALM 148:12–14

This people I have formed for Myself;
They shall declare My praise.

ISAIAH 43:21

Praise the LORD!
Praise God in His sanctuary;
Praise Him in His mighty firmament!
Praise Him for His mighty acts;
Praise Him according to His excellent
    greatness!
Praise Him with the sound of the trumpet;
Praise Him with the lute and harp!
Praise Him with the timbrel and dance;
Praise Him with stringed instruments
    and flutes!
Praise Him with loud cymbals;
Praise Him with clashing cymbals!
Let everything that has breath praise
    the LORD.
Praise the LORD!

PSALM 150:1–6

I will call upon the LORD, who is worthy
    to be praised;
So shall I be saved from my enemies.

2 SAMUEL 22:4

But you are a chosen generation, a royal priesthood, a holy nation, His own special people, that you may proclaim the praises of Him who called you out of darkness into His marvelous light.

1 PETER 2:9

> May the LORD give you increase more
>   and more,
> You and your children.
> May you be blessed by the LORD,
> Who made heaven and earth.
> The heaven, even the heavens, are
>   the LORD's;
> But the earth He has given to the children
>   of men.
> The dead do not praise the LORD,
> Nor any who go down into silence.
> But we will bless the LORD
> From this time forth and forevermore.
> Praise the LORD!

PSALM 115:14–18

Know that the LORD, He is God;
It is He who has made us, and not we ourselves;
We are His people and the sheep of His pasture.
Enter into His gates with thanksgiving,
And into His courts with praise.
Be thankful to Him, and bless His name.
For the LORD is good;
His mercy is everlasting,
And His truth endures to all generations.

PSALM 100:3–5

I will sing of the mercies of the LORD forever;
With my mouth will I make known Your
            faithfulness to all generations.
For I have said, "Mercy shall be built up
            forever;
Your faithfulness You shall establish in the
            very heavens."
"I have made a covenant with My chosen,
I have sworn to My servant David:
'Your seed I will establish forever,
And build up your throne to all generations.' "

PSALM 89:1–4

I thank You and praise You,
O God of my fathers;
You have given me wisdom and might,
And have now made known to me what we
     asked of You,
For You have made known to us the king's
     demand.

DANIEL 2:23

I love those who love me,
And those who seek me diligently will
find me.

PROVERBS 8:17

You are the salt of the earth; but if the salt loses its flavor, how shall it be seasoned? It is then good for nothing but to be thrown out and trampled underfoot by men.

You are the light of the world. A city that is set on a hill cannot be hidden. Nor do they light a lamp and put it under a basket, but on a lampstand, and it gives light to all who are in the house. Let your light so shine before men, that they may see your good works and glorify your Father in heaven.

MATTHEW 5:13–16

That Christ may dwell in your hearts through faith; that you, being rooted and grounded in love, may be able to comprehend with all the saints what is the width and length and depth and height— to know the love of Christ which passes knowledge; that you may be filled with all the fullness of God.

EPHESIANS 3:17–19

"At the same time," says the LORD, "I will be the God of all the families of Israel, and they shall be My people."

Thus says the LORD:
"The people who survived the sword
Found grace in the wilderness—
Israel, when I went to give him rest."
The LORD has appeared of old to me, saying:
"Yes, I have loved you with an everlasting love;
Therefore with lovingkindness I have drawn you."
JEREMIAH 31:1–3

And you shall love the LORD your God with all your heart, with all your soul, with all your mind, and with all your strength. This is the first commandment.
MARK 12:30

As the Father loved Me, I also have loved you; abide in My love. If you keep My commandments, you will abide in My love, just as I have kept My Father's commandments and abide in His love.
JOHN 15:9–10

Then we cried out to the LORD God of our fathers, and the LORD heard our voice and looked on our affliction and our labor and our oppression. So the LORD brought us out of Egypt with a mighty hand and with an outstretched arm, with great terror and with signs and wonders. He has brought us to this place and has given us this land, a land flowing with milk and honey; and now, behold, I have brought the firstfruits of the land which you, O LORD, have given me. Then you shall set it before the LORD your God, and worship before the LORD your God.

DEUTERONOMY 26:7–10

Make a joyful shout to the LORD, all
    you lands!
Serve the LORD with gladness;
Come before His presence with singing.

PSALM 100:1–2

Then Jesus said to him, "Away with you, Satan! For it is written, 'You shall worship the Lord your God, and Him only you shall serve.' "

MATTHEW 4:10

The LORD lives!
Blessed be my Rock!
Let God be exalted,
The Rock of my salvation!

2 SAMUEL 22:47

Let them give glory to the LORD,
And declare His praise in the coastlands.

ISAIAH 42:12

Let the word of Christ dwell in you richly in all wisdom,
teaching and admonishing one another in psalms and
hymns and spiritual songs, singing with grace in your
hearts to the Lord.

COLOSSIANS 3:16

Give to the LORD the glory due His name;
Bring an offering, and come before Him.
Oh, worship the LORD in the beauty of holiness!

1 CHRONICLES 16:29

Also with the lute I will praise you—
And Your faithfulness, O my God!
To You I will sing with the harp,
O Holy One of Israel.
My lips shall greatly rejoice when I sing to You,
And my soul, which You have redeemed.
My tongue also shall talk of Your
      righteousness all the day long;
For they are confounded,
For they are brought to shame
Who seek my hurt.

PSALM 71:22–24

God Keeps a Man
Secure When . . .

— ❧❧ —

Therefore humble yourselves under the mighty hand
of God, that He may exalt you in due time, casting all
your care upon Him, for He cares for you.

1 PETER 5:6–7

> My son, if you receive my words,
> And treasure my commands within you,
> So that you incline your ear to wisdom,
> And apply your heart to understanding;
> Yes, if you cry out for discernment,
> And lift up your voice for understanding,
> If you seek her as silver,
> And search for her as for hidden treasures;
> Then you will understand the fear of
>   the LORD,
> And find the knowledge of God.

PROVERBS 2:1–5

Be strong and of good courage, do not fear nor be
afraid of them; for the LORD your God, He is the
One who goes with you. He will not leave you nor
forsake you.

DEUTERONOMY 31:6

Then the king arose very early in the morning and went in haste to the den of lions. And when he came to the den, he cried out with a lamenting voice to Daniel. The king spoke, saying to Daniel, "Daniel, servant of the living God, has your God, whom you serve continually, been able to deliver you from the lions?"

Then Daniel said to the king, "O king, live forever! My God sent His angel and shut the lions' mouths, so that they have not hurt me, because I was found innocent before Him; and also, O king, I have done no wrong before you."

DANIEL 6:19–22

I will love You, O LORD, my strength.
The LORD is my rock and my fortress
and my deliverer;
My God, my strength, in whom I will trust;
My shield and the horn of my salvation,
my stronghold.
I will call upon the LORD, who is worthy
to be praised;
So shall I be saved from my enemies.

PSALM 18:1–3

Therefore submit to God. Resist the devil and he will flee from you. Draw near to God and He will draw near to you. Cleanse your hands, you sinners; and purify your hearts, you double-minded.

JAMES 4:7–8

This Book of the Law shall not depart from your mouth, but you shall meditate in it day and night, that you may observe to do according to all that is written in it. For then you will make your way prosperous, and then you will have good success. Have I not commanded you? Be strong and of good courage; do not be afraid, nor be dismayed, for the LORD your God is with you wherever you go.

JOSHUA 1:8–9

When wisdom enters your heart,
And knowledge is pleasant to your soul,
Discretion will preserve you;
Understanding will keep you,
To deliver you from the way of evil,
From the man who speaks perverse things.

PROVERBS 2:10–12

For the Scripture says, "You shall not muzzle an ox while it treads out the grain," and, "The laborer is worthy of his wages."

1 TIMOTHY 5:18

What profit has the worker from that in which he labors? I have seen the God-given task with which the sons of men are to be occupied. He has made everything beautiful in its time. Also He has put eternity in their hearts, except that no one can find out the work that God does from beginning to end.

I know that nothing is better for them than to rejoice, and to do good in their lives, and also that every man should eat and drink and enjoy the good of all his labor—it is the gift of God.

ECCLESIASTES 3:9–13

Do not overwork to be rich;
Because of your own understanding, cease!
Will you set your eyes on that which is not?
For riches certainly make themselves wings;
They fly away like an eagle toward heaven.

PROVERBS 23:4–5

145

Then I hated all my labor in which I had toiled under the sun, because I must leave it to the man who will come after me. And who knows whether he will be wise or a fool? Yet he will rule over all my labor in which I toiled and in which I have shown myself wise under the sun. This also is vanity. Therefore I turned my heart and despaired of all the labor in which I had toiled under the sun.

For God gives wisdom and knowledge and joy to a man who is good in His sight; but to the sinner He gives the work of gathering and collecting, that he may give to him who is good before God. This also is vanity and grasping for the wind.

ECCLESIASTES 2:18–20, 26

For no other foundation can anyone lay than that which is laid, which is Jesus Christ. Now if anyone builds on this foundation with gold, silver, precious stones, wood, hay, straw, each one's work will become clear; for the Day will declare it, because it will be revealed by fire; and the fire will test each one's work, of what sort it is. If anyone's work which he has built on it endures, he will receive a reward. If anyone's work is burned, he will suffer loss; but he himself will be saved, yet so as through fire.

1 CORINTHIANS 3:11–15

Therefore I say to you, do not worry about your life, what you will eat or what you will drink; nor about your body, what you will put on. Is not life more than food and the body more than clothing? Look at the birds of the air, for they neither sow nor reap nor gather into barns; yet your heavenly Father feeds them. Are you not of more value than they? Which of you by worrying can add one cubit to his stature?

So why do you worry about clothing? Consider the lilies of the field, how they grow: they neither toil nor spin; and yet I say to you that even Solomon in all his glory was not arrayed like one of these. Now if God so clothes the grass of the field, which today is, and tomorrow is thrown into the oven, will He not much more clothe you, O you of little faith?

Therefore do not worry, saying, "What shall we eat?" or "What shall we drink?" or "What shall we wear?" For after all these things the Gentiles seek. For your heavenly Father knows that you need all these things. But seek first the kingdom of God and His righteousness, and all these things shall be added to you. Therefore do not worry about tomorrow, for tomorrow will worry about its own things. Sufficient for the day is its own trouble.

MATTHEW 6:25–34

The name of the LORD is a strong tower;
The righteous run to it and are safe.

PROVERBS 18:10

Do not put your trust in princes,
Nor in a son of man, in whom there is
    no help.
His spirit departs, he returns to his earth;
In that very day his plans perish.
Happy is he who has the God of Jacob for
    his help,
Whose hope is in the LORD his God.

PSALM 146:3–5

You will keep him in perfect peace,
Whose mind is stayed on You,
Because he trusts in You.

ISAIAH 26:3

The eyes of all look expectantly to You,
And You give them their food in due season.
You open Your hand
And satisfy the desire of every living thing.
The LORD is righteous in all His ways,
Gracious in all His works.
The LORD is near to all who call upon Him,
To all who call upon Him in truth.
He will fulfill the desire of those who fear Him;
He also will hear their cry and save them.
The LORD preserves all who love Him,
But all the wicked He will destroy.
My mouth shall speak the praise of the LORD,
And all flesh shall bless His holy name
Forever and ever.

PSALM 145:15–21

The work of righteousness will be peace,
And the effect of righteousness, quietness
      and assurance forever.

                ISAIAH 32:17

I will both lie down in peace, and sleep;
For You alone, O LORD, make me dwell
      in safety.

                PSALM 4:8

Blessed is every one who fears the LORD,
Who walks in His ways.
When you eat the labor of your hands,
You shall be happy, and it shall be well
      with you.
Your wife shall be like a fruitful vine
In the very heart of your house,
Your children like olive plants
All around your table.
Behold, thus shall the man be blessed
Who fears the LORD.
The LORD bless you out of Zion,
And may you see the good of Jerusalem
All the days of your life.
Yes, may you see your children's children.
Peace be upon Israel!

              PSALM 128:1–6

For I will pour water on him who is thirsty,
And floods on the dry ground;
I will pour My Spirit on your descendants,
And My blessing on your offspring.

ISAIAH 44:3

But because the LORD loves you, and because He would keep the oath which He swore to your fathers, the LORD has brought you out with a mighty hand, and redeemed you from the house of bondage, from the hand of Pharaoh king of Egypt.

Therefore know that the LORD your God, He is God, the faithful God who keeps covenant and mercy for a thousand generations with those who love Him and keep His commandments.

DEUTERONOMY 7:8–9

Your mercy, O LORD, is in the heavens;
Your faithfulness reaches to the clouds.

PSALM 36:5

Blessed be the LORD,
Who daily loads us with benefits,
The God of our salvation!

PSALM 68:19

The father of the righteous will greatly
    rejoice,
And he who begets a wise child will
    delight in him.
Let your father and your mother be glad,
And let her who bore you rejoice.
My son, give me your heart,
And let your eyes observe my ways.

PROVERBS 23:24–26

The young lions lack and suffer hunger;
But those who seek the LORD shall not
    lack any good thing.

PSALM 34:10

The humble shall see this and be glad;
And you who seek God, your hearts shall live.
For the LORD hears the poor,
And does not despise His prisoners.
Let heaven and earth praise Him,
The seas and everything that moves in them.

PSALM 69:32–34

The LORD will command the blessing on you in your storehouses and in all to which you set your hand, and He will bless you in the land which the LORD your God is giving you.

DEUTERONOMY 28:8

You shall eat in plenty and be satisfied,
And praise the name of the LORD your God,
Who has dealt wondrously with you;
And My people shall never be put to shame.

JOEL 2:26

The poor and needy seek water, but there
    is none,
Their tongues fail for thirst.
I, the LORD, will hear them;
I, the God of Israel, will not forsake them.

                        ISAIAH 41:17

Come to the waters;
And you who have no money,
Come, buy and eat.
Yes, come, buy wine and milk
Without money and without price.
Why do you spend money for what is
    not bread,
And your wages for what does not satisfy?
Listen carefully to Me, and eat what is good,
And let your soul delight itself in abundance.
Incline your ear, and come to Me.
Hear, and your soul shall live;
And I will make an everlasting covenant
    with you—
The sure mercies of David.

                        ISAIAH 55:1–3

God's Promises

I have been young, and now am old;
Yet I have not seen the righteous forsaken,
Nor his descendants begging bread.
He is ever merciful, and lends;
And his descendants are blessed.
Depart from evil, and do good;
And dwell forevermore.
For the LORD loves justice,
And does not forsake His saints;
They are preserved forever,
But the descendants of the wicked shall
        be cut off.

PSALM 37:25–28

And my God shall supply all your need according to
His riches in glory by Christ Jesus.

PHILIPPIANS 4:19

I will satiate the soul of the priests with
        abundance,
And My people shall be satisfied with My
        goodness, says the LORD.

JEREMIAH 31:14

GOD COMFORTS
A MAN WHEN . . .

———— ✄✄ ————

For the LORD God will help Me;
Therefore I will not be disgraced;
Therefore I have set My face like a flint,
And I know that I will not be ashamed.

ISAIAH 50:7

Come to Me, all you who labor and are heavy laden, and I will give you rest. Take My yoke upon you and learn from Me, for I am gentle and lowly in heart, and you will find rest for your souls. For My yoke is easy and My burden is light.

MATTHEW 11:28–30

For the eyes of the LORD run to and fro throughout the whole earth, to show Himself strong on behalf of those whose heart is loyal to Him.

2 CHRONICLES 16:9

"I will be a Father to you, and you shall be My sons and daughters," says the Lord Almighty.

2 CORINTHIANS 6:18

Not that we are sufficient of ourselves to think of anything as being from ourselves, but our sufficiency is
from God.

2 CORINTHIANS 3:5

> LORD, my heart is not haughty,
> Nor my eyes lofty.
> Neither do I concern myself with great matters,
> Nor with things too profound for me.
> Surely I have calmed and quieted my soul,
> Like a weaned child with his mother;
> Like a weaned child is my soul within me.
> O Israel, hope in the LORD
> From this time forth and forever.
>
> PSALM 131:1–3

But by the grace of God I am what I am, and His
grace toward me was not in vain; but I labored more
abundantly than they all, yet not I, but the grace of
God which was with me. Therefore, whether it was I
or they, so we preach and so you believed.

1 CORINTHIANS 15:10–11

I have blotted out, like a thick cloud,
> your transgressions,
And like a cloud, your sins.
Return to Me, for I have redeemed you.

ISAIAH 44:22

By which have been given to us exceedingly great and precious promises, that through these you may be partakers of the divine nature, having escaped the corruption that is in the world through lust.

But also for this very reason, giving all diligence, add to your faith virtue, to virtue knowledge, to knowledge self-control, to self-control perseverance, to perseverance godliness, to godliness brotherly kindness, and to brotherly kindness love. For if these things are yours and abound, you will be neither barren nor unfruitful in the knowledge of our Lord Jesus Christ.

2 PETER 1:4–8

Beloved, I pray that you may prosper in all things and be in health, just as your soul prospers.

3 JOHN 2

Jesus said to him, "If you can believe, all things are possible to him who believes."

Immediately the father of the child cried out and said with tears, "Lord, I believe; help my unbelief!"

MARK 9:23–24

When Jesus came into the ruler's house, and saw the flute players and the noisy crowd wailing, He said to them, "Make room, for the girl is not dead, but sleeping." And they ridiculed Him. But when the crowd was put outside, He went in and took her by the hand, and the girl arose. And the report of this went out into all that land.

MATTHEW 9:23–26

Who Himself bore our sins in His own body on the tree, that we, having died to sins, might live for righteousness—by whose stripes you were healed.

1 PETER 2:24

But He was wounded for our transgressions,
He was bruised for our iniquities;
The chastisement for our peace was
    upon Him,
And by His stripes we are healed.

ISAIAH 53:5

Is anyone among you sick? Let him call for the elders of the church, and let them pray over him, anointing him with oil in the name of the Lord. And the prayer of faith will save the sick, and the Lord will raise him up. And if he has committed sins, he will be forgiven. Confess your trespasses to one another, and pray for one another, that you may be healed. The effective, fervent prayer of a righteous man avails much.

JAMES 5:14–16

Heal me, O LORD, and I shall be healed;
Save me, and I shall be saved,
For You are my praise.

JEREMIAH 17:14

"For I will restore health to you
And heal you of your wounds," says
    the LORD.

JEREMIAH 30:17A

If you diligently heed the voice of the LORD your God and do what is right in His sight, give ear to His commandments and keep all His statutes, I will put none of the diseases on you which I have brought on the Egyptians. For I am the LORD who heals you.

EXODUS 15:26

My son, give attention to my words;
Incline your ear to my sayings.
Do not let them depart from your eyes;
Keep them in the midst of your heart;
For they are life to those who find them,
And health to all their flesh.

PROVERBS 4:20–22

GOD COMFORTS A MAN WHEN . . . HIS LOVED ONES DON'T UNDERSTAND HIM

Let love be without hypocrisy. Abhor what is evil. Cling to what is good. Be kindly affectionate to one another with brotherly love, in honor giving preference to one another.

ROMANS 12:9–10

A word fitly spoken is like apples of gold
In settings of silver.
By long forbearance a ruler is persuaded,
And a gentle tongue breaks a bone.

PROVERBS 25:11, 15

Though I speak with the tongues of men and of angels, but have not love, I have become sounding brass or a clanging cymbal. And though I have the gift of prophecy, and understand all mysteries and all knowledge, and though I have all faith, so that I could remove mountains, but have not love, I am nothing. And though I bestow all my goods to feed the poor, and though I give my body to be burned, but have not love, it profits me nothing.

1 CORINTHIANS 13:1–3

Great is our LORD, and mighty in power; His understanding is infinite.

PSALM 147:5

For if you love those who love you, what reward have you? Do not even the tax collectors do the same? And if you greet your brethren only, what do you do more than others? Do not even the tax collectors do so? Therefore you shall be perfect, just as your Father in heaven is perfect.

MATTHEW 5:46–48

Finally, all of you be of one mind, having compassion for one another; love as brothers, be tenderhearted, be courteous; not returning evil for evil or reviling for reviling, but on the contrary blessing, knowing that you were called to this, that you may inherit a blessing. For

> "He who would love life
> And see good days,
> Let him refrain his tongue from evil,
> And his lips from speaking deceit.
> Let him turn away from evil and do good;
> Let him seek peace and pursue it."

1 PETER 3:8–11

My son, do not despise the chastening of
the LORD,
Nor detest His correction;
For whom the LORD loves He corrects,
Just as a father the son in whom he delights.

PROVERBS 3:11–12

Furthermore, we have had human fathers who corrected us, and we paid them respect. Shall we not much more readily be in subjection to the Father of spirits and live? For they indeed for a few days chastened us as seemed best to them, but He for our profit, that we may be partakers of His holiness. Now no chastening seems to be joyful for the present, but painful; nevertheless, afterward it yields the peaceable fruit of righteousness to those who have been trained by it.

HEBREWS 12:9–11

The rod and rebuke give wisdom,
But a child left to himself brings shame to
his mother.
Correct your son, and he will give you rest;
Yes, he will give delight to your soul.

PROVERBS 29:15, 17

Now I rejoice, not that you were made sorry, but that your sorrow led to repentance. For you were made sorry in a godly manner, that you might suffer loss from us in nothing.

2 CORINTHIANS 7:9

Chasten your son while there is hope,
And do not set your heart on his destruction.

PROVERBS 19:18

Hatred stirs up strife,
But love covers all sins.
Wisdom is found on the lips of him who
    has understanding,
But a rod is for the back of him who
    is devoid of understanding.

PROVERBS 10:12–13

Whoever loves instruction loves knowledge,
But he who hates correction is stupid.
A good man obtains favor from the LORD,
But a man of wicked intentions He will
    condemn.
A man is not established by wickedness,
But the root of the righteous cannot
    be moved.

PROVERBS 12:1–3

Therefore be very courageous to keep and to do all that is written in the Book of the Law of Moses, lest you turn aside from it to the right hand or to the left, . . .

But you shall hold fast to the LORD your God, as you have done to this day.

JOSHUA 23:6, 8

My son, keep my words,
And treasure my commands within you.
Keep my commands and live,
And my law as the apple of your eye.
Bind them on your fingers;
Write them on the tablet of your heart.

PROVERBS 7:1–3

My son, if you receive my words,
And treasure my commands within you,
So that you incline your ear to wisdom,
And apply your heart to understanding;
Yes, if you cry out for discernment,
And lift up your voice for understanding,
If you seek her as silver,
And search for her as for hidden treasures;
Then you will understand the fear of
    the LORD,
And find the knowledge of God.
For the LORD gives wisdom;
From His mouth come knowledge
    and understanding;
He stores up sound wisdom for the upright;
He is a shield to those who walk uprightly;
He guards the paths of justice,
And preserves the way of His saints.
Then you will understand righteousness
    and justice,
Equity and every good path.

PROVERBS 2:1–9

In the fear of the LORD there is strong
      confidence,
And His children will have a place of refuge.
The fear of the LORD is a fountain of life,
To turn one away from the snares of death.

                PROVERBS 14:26–27

In the way of righteousness is life,
And in its pathway there is no death.

                PROVERBS 12:28

Wine is a mocker,
Strong drink is a brawler,
And whoever is led astray by it is not wise.

                PROVERBS 20:1

He who loves pleasure will be a poor man;
He who loves wine and oil will not be rich.

                PROVERBS 21:17

In mercy and truth
Atonement is provided for iniquity;
And by the fear of the LORD one departs
      from evil.

                PROVERBS 16:6

Do you not know that you are the temple of God and that the Spirit of God dwells in you? If anyone defiles the temple of God, God will destroy him. For the temple of God is holy, which temple you are.

1 CORINTHIANS 3:16–17

And do not fear those who kill the body but cannot kill the soul. But rather fear Him who is able to destroy both soul and body in hell.

MATTHEW 10:28

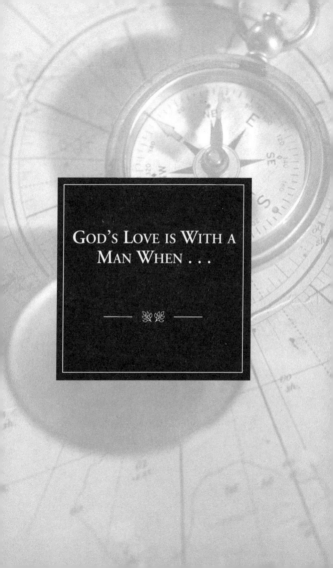

God's Love is With a
Man When . . .

❧❧

If you would prepare your heart,
And stretch out your hands toward Him;
If iniquity were in your hand, and you put
    it far away,
And would not let wickedness dwell in
    your tents;
Then surely you could lift up your face
    without spot;
Yes, you could be steadfast, and not fear;
Because you would forget your misery,
And remember it as waters that have
    passed away,
And your life would be brighter than
    noonday.
Though you were dark, you would be
    like the morning.
And you would be secure, because there
    is hope;
Yes, you would dig around you, and
    take your rest in safety.

JOB 11:13–18

But Jesus looked at them and said to them, "With men this is impossible, but with God all things are possible."

MATTHEW 19:26

Blessed be the LORD, who has given rest to His people Israel, according to all that He promised. There has not failed one word of all His good promise, which He promised through His servant Moses. May the LORD our God be with us, as He was with our fathers. May He not leave us nor forsake us, that He may incline our hearts to Himself, to walk in all His ways, and to keep His commandments and His statutes and His judgments, which He commanded our fathers. And may these words of mine, with which I have made supplication before the LORD, be near the LORD our God day and night, that He may maintain the cause of His servant and the cause of His people Israel, as each day may require.

1 KINGS 8:56–59

Yes, we had the sentence of death in ourselves, that we should not trust in ourselves but in God who raises the dead, who delivered us from so great a death, and does deliver us; in whom we trust that He will still deliver us.

2 CORINTHIANS 1:9–10

For the eyes of the LORD are on the righteous,
And His ears are open to their prayers;
But the face of the LORD is against those
    who do evil.

And who is he who will harm you if you become followers of what is good? But even if you should suffer for righteousness' sake, you are blessed. And do not be afraid of their threats, nor be troubled. But sanctify the Lord God in your hearts, and always be ready to give a defense to everyone who asks you a reason for the hope that is in you, with meekness and fear.

1 PETER 3:12–15

You have made the heavens and the earth by Your great power and outstreached arm. There is nothing too hard for You.

JEREMIAH 32:17

Consider what I say, and may the Lord give you understanding in all things. This is a faithful saying:

For if we died with Him,
We shall also live with Him.
If we endure,
We shall also reign with Him.
If we deny Him,
He also will deny us.

2 TIMOTHY 2:7, 11–12

And to give you who are troubled rest with us when the Lord Jesus is revealed from heaven with His mighty angels, in flaming fire taking vengeance on those who do not know God, and on those who do not obey the gospel of our Lord Jesus Christ. These shall be punished with everlasting destruction from the presence of the Lord and from the glory of His power, when He comes, in that Day, to be glorified in His saints and to be admired among all those who believe, because our testimony among you was believed.

Therefore we also pray always for you that our God would count you worthy of this calling, and fulfill all the good pleasure of His goodness and the work of faith with power, that the name of our Lord Jesus Christ may be glorified in you, and you in Him, according to the grace of our God and the Lord Jesus Christ.

2 THESSALONIANS 1:7–12

God is my strength and power, and He makes my way perfect.

2 SAMUEL 22:33

In Your hand is power and might; in Your hand it is to make great and to give strength to all.

1 CHRONICLES 29:12

The Spirit of the Lord GOD is upon Me,
Because the LORD has anointed Me
To preach good tidings to the poor;
He has sent Me to heal the brokenhearted,
To proclaim liberty to the captives,
And the opening of the prison to those
     who are bound;
To proclaim the acceptable year of the LORD,
And the day of vengeance of our God;
To comfort all who mourn,
To console those who mourn in Zion,
To give them beauty for ashes,
The oil of joy for mourning,
The garment of praise for the spirit
     of heaviness;
That they may be called trees of righteousness,
The planting of the LORD, that He may
     be glorified.

ISAIAH 61:1–3

We are hard pressed on every side, yet not crushed; we are perplexed, but not in despair; persecuted, but not forsaken; struck down, but not destroyed—always carrying about in the body the dying of the Lord Jesus, that the life of Jesus also may be manifested in our body.

For all things are for your sakes, that grace, having spread through the many, may cause thanksgiving to abound to the glory of God.

Therefore we do not lose heart. Even though our outward man is perishing, yet the inward man is being renewed day by day. For our light affliction, which is but for a moment, is working for us a far more exceeding and eternal weight of glory, while we do not look at the things which are seen, but at the things which are not seen. For the things which are seen are temporary, but the things which are not seen are eternal.

2 CORINTHIANS 4;8–10, 15–18

Now thanks be to God who always leads us in triumph in Christ, and through us diffuses the fragrance of His knowledge in every place. For we are to God the fragrance of Christ among those being saved and among those who are perishing. To the one we are the aroma of death leading to death, and to the other the aroma of life leading to life. And who is sufficient for these things? For we are not, as so many, peddling the word of God; but as of sincerity, but as from God we speak in the sight of God in Christ.

2 CORINTHIANS 2:14–17

My little children, these things I write to you, so that you may not sin. And if anyone sins, we have an Advocate with the Father, Jesus Christ the righteous.

1 JOHN 2:1

The Son of Man has come to seek and to save that which was lost.

LUKE 19:10

I will go before you
And make the crooked places straight;
I will break in pieces the gates of bronze
And cut the bars of iron.
I will give you the treasures of darkness
And hidden riches of secret places,
That you may know that I, the LORD,
Who call you by your name,
Am the God of Israel.

ISAIAH 45:2–3

Have you not known?
Have you not heard?
The everlasting God, the LORD,
The Creator of the ends of the earth,
Neither faints nor is weary.
His understanding is unsearchable.
He gives power to the weak,
And to those who have no might He
      increases strength.
Even the youths shall faint and be weary,
And the young men shall utterly fall,
But those who wait on the LORD
Shall renew their strength;
They shall mount up with wings like eagles,
They shall run and not be weary,
They shall walk and not faint.

ISAIAH 40:28–31

When you roam, they will lead you;
When you sleep, they will keep you;
And when you awake, they will speak
      with you.
For the commandment is a lamp,
And the law a light;
Reproofs of instruction are the way of life.

PROVERBS 6:22–23

Do not remember the former things,
Nor consider the things of old.
Behold, I will do a new thing,
Now it shall spring forth;
Shall you not know it?
I will even make a road in the wilderness
And rivers in the desert.

ISAIAH 43:18–19

Fear not, for I am with you;
Be not dismayed, for I am your God.
I will strengthen you,
Yes, I will help you,
I will uphold you with My righteous right hand.

ISAIAH 41:10

"I have made the earth,
And created man on it.
I—My hands— stretched out the heavens,
And all their host I have commanded.
I have raised him up in righteousness,
And I will direct all his ways;
He shall build My city
And let My exiles go free,
Not for price nor reward,"
Says the LORD of hosts.

ISAIAH 45:12–13

For as the rain comes down, and the
    snow from heaven,
And do not return there,
But water the earth,
And make it bring forth and bud,
That it may give seed to the sower
And bread to the eater,
So shall My word be that goes forth from
    My mouth;
It shall not return to Me void,
But it shall accomplish what I please,
And it shall prosper in the thing for which
    I sent it.

ISAIAH 55:10–11

You have been my defense and refuge in the day of my trouble.

PSALM 59:16

"For the mountains shall depart
And the hills be removed,
But My kindness shall not depart from you,
Nor shall My covenant of peace
    be removed,"
Says the LORD, who has mercy on you.

ISAIAH 54:10

You shall surely give to him, and your heart should not be grieved when you give to him, because for this thing the LORD your God will bless you in all your works and in all to which you put your hand. For the poor will never cease from the land; therefore I command you, saying, "You shall open your hand wide to your brother, to your poor and your needy, in your land."

DEUTERONOMY 15:10–11

> The LORD makes poor and makes rich;
> He brings low and lifts up.
> He raises the poor from the dust
> And lifts the beggar from the ash heap,
> To set them among princes
> And make them inherit the throne of glory.
> For the pillars of the earth are the LORD's,
> And He has set the world upon them.

1 SAMUEL 2:7–8

Give, and it will be given to you: good measure, pressed down, shaken together, and running over will be put into your bosom.

LUKE 6:38

He who oppresses the poor reproaches
    his Maker,
But he who honors Him has mercy on
    the needy.

PROVERBS 14:31

Now the multitude of those who believed were of one heart and one soul; neither did anyone say that any of the things he possessed was his own, but they had all things in common. And with great power the apostles gave witness to the resurrection of the LORD Jesus. And great grace was upon them all. Nor was there anyone among them who lacked; for all who were possessors of lands or houses sold them, and brought the proceeds of the things that were sold, and laid them at the apostles' feet; and they distributed to each as anyone had need.

ACTS 4:32–35

He who mocks the poor reproaches his Maker;
He who is glad at calamity will not
    go unpunished.

PROVERBS 17:5

It is more blessed to give than to receive.

ACTS 20:35

What does it profit, my brethren, if someone says he has faith but does not have works? Can faith save him? If a brother or sister is naked and destitute of daily food, and one of you says to them, "Depart in peace, be warmed and filled," but you do not give them the things which are needed for the body, what does it profit? Thus also faith by itself, if it does not have works, is dead.

JAMES 2:14–17

Jesus said to him, "If you want to be perfect, go, sell what you have and give to the poor, and you will have treasure in heaven; and come, follow Me."

But when the young man heard that saying, he went away sorrowful, for he had great possessions.

Then Jesus said to His disciples, "Assuredly, I say to you that it is hard for a rich man to enter the kingdom of heaven. And again I say to you, it is easier for a camel to go through the eye of a needle than for a rich man to enter the kingdom of God."

MATTHEW 19:21–24

Delight yourself also in the LORD,
And He shall give you the desires of
    your heart.

PSALM 37:4

The LORD is near to all who call upon Him,
To all who call upon Him in truth.
He will fulfill the desire of those who
    fear Him;
He also will hear their cry and save them.

PSALM 145:18–19

Rejoice in the Lord always. Again I will say, rejoice!

Let your gentleness be known to all men. The Lord is at hand.

Be anxious for nothing, but in everything by prayer and supplication, with thanksgiving, let your requests be made known to God; and the peace of God, which surpasses all understanding, will guard your hearts and minds through Christ Jesus.

PHILIPPIANS 4:4–7

Call to Me, and I will answer you, and show you great and mighty things, which you do not know.

JEREMIAH 33:3

You also helping together in prayer for us, that thanks may be given by many persons on our behalf for the gift granted to us through many.

For our boasting is this: the testimony of our conscience that we conducted ourselves in the world in simplicity and godly sincerity, not with fleshly wisdom but by the grace of God, and more abundantly toward you. For we are not writing any other things to you than what you read or understand. Now I trust you will understand, even to the end (as also you have understood us in part), that we are your boast as you also are ours, in the day of the Lord Jesus.

2 CORINTHIANS 1:11–14

And whatever things you ask in prayer, believing, you will receive.

MATTHEW 21:22

Again I say to you that if two of you agree on earth concerning anything that they ask, it will be done for them by My Father in heaven. For where two or three are gathered together in My name, I am there in the midst of them.

MATTHEW 18:19–20

Let us therefore come boldly to the throne of grace, that we may obtain mercy and find grace to help in time of need.

HEBREWS 4:16

Then I set my face toward the Lord God to make request by prayer and supplications, with fasting, sackcloth, and ashes. And I prayed to the LORD my God, and made confession, and said, "O Lord, great and awesome God, who keeps His covenant and mercy with those who love Him, and with those who keep His commandments, we have sinned and committed iniquity, we have done wickedly and rebelled, even by departing from Your precepts and Your judgments."

"Now therefore, our God, hear the prayer of Your servant, and his supplications, and for the Lord's sake cause Your face to shine on Your sanctuary, which is desolate. O my God, incline Your ear and hear; open Your eyes and see our desolations, and the city which is called by Your name; for we do not present our supplications before You because of our righteous deeds, but because of Your great mercies."

DANIEL 9:3–5, 17–18

Then Peter came to Him and said, "Lord, how often shall my brother sin against me, and I forgive him? Up to seven times?"

Jesus said to him, "I do not say to you, up to seven times, but up to seventy times seven."

MATTHEW 18:21–22

But love your enemies, do good, and lend, hoping for nothing in return; and your reward will be great, and you will be sons of the Most High. For He is kind to the unthankful and evil. Therefore be merciful, just as your Father also is merciful.

Judge not, and you shall not be judged. Condemn not, and you shall not be condemned. Forgive, and you will be forgiven.

LUKE 6:35–37

For if you forgive men their trespasses, your heavenly Father will also forgive you. But if you do not forgive men their trespasses, neither will your Father forgive your trespasses.

MATTHEW 6:14–15

He made known His ways to Moses,
His acts to the children of Israel.
The LORD is merciful and gracious,
Slow to anger, and abounding in mercy.
He will not always strive with us,
Nor will He keep His anger forever.
He has not dealt with us according to our sins,
Nor punished us according to our iniquities.
For as the heavens are high above the earth,
So great is His mercy toward those who
     fear Him;
As far as the east is from the west,
So far has He removed our transgressions
     from us.
As a father pities his children,
So the LORD pities those who fear Him.

PSALM 103:7–13

Take heed to yourselves. If your brother sins against
you, rebuke him; and if he repents, forgive him. And
if he sins against you seven times in a day, and seven
times in a day returns to you, saying, "I repent" you
shall forgive him."

LUKE 17:3–4

Whenever you stand praying, if you have anything against anyone, forgive him, that your Father in heaven may also forgive you your trespasses. But if you do not forgive, neither will your Father in heaven forgive your trespasses.

MARK 11:25–26

GOD REJOICES
WHEN A MAN . . .

—— ❧❧ ——

GOD REJOICES WHEN A MAN ANTICIPATES CHRIST'S RETURN

Behold what manner of love the Father has bestowed on us, that we should be called children of God! Therefore the world does not know us, because it did not know Him. Beloved, now we are children of God; and it has not yet been revealed what we shall be, but we know that when He is revealed, we shall be like Him, for we shall see Him as He is. And everyone who has this hope in Him purifies himself, just as He is pure.

1 JOHN 3:1–3

Let not your heart be troubled; you believe in God, believe also in Me. In My Father's house are many mansions; if it were not so, I would have told you. I go to prepare a place for you. And if I go and prepare a place for you, I will come again and receive you to Myself; that where I am, there you may be also.

JOHN 14:1–3

So the ransomed of the LORD shall return,
And come to Zion with singing,
With everlasting joy on their heads.
They shall obtain joy and gladness;
Sorrow and sighing shall flee away.

ISAIAH 51:11

For behold, I create new heavens and a
    new earth;
And the former shall not be remembered
    or come to mind.
But be glad and rejoice forever in what I create;
For behold, I create Jerusalem as a rejoicing,
And her people a joy.
I will rejoice in Jerusalem,
And joy in My people;
The voice of weeping shall no longer
    be heard in her,
Nor the voice of crying.

ISAIAH 65:17–19

There will be signs in the sun, in the moon, and in
the stars; and on the earth distress of nations, with
perplexity, the sea and the waves roaring; men's hearts
failing them from fear and the expectation of those
things which are coming on the earth, for the powers
of the heavens will be shaken. Then they will see the
Son of Man coming in a cloud with power and great
glory. Now when these things begin to happen, look
up and lift up your heads, because your redemption
draws near.

LUKE 21:25–28

For as the lightning comes from the east and flashes to the west, so also will the coming of the Son of Man be. For wherever the carcass is, there the eagles will be gathered together.

Immediately after the tribulation of those days the sun will be darkened, and the moon will not give its light; the stars will fall from heaven, and the powers of the heavens will be shaken. Then the sign of the Son of Man will appear in heaven, and then all the tribes of the earth will mourn, and they will see the Son of Man coming on the clouds of heaven with power and great glory. And He will send His angels with a great sound of a trumpet, and they will gather together His elect from the four winds, from one end of heaven to the other.

MATTHEW 24:27–31

The day of the Lord will come as a thief in the night, in which the heavens will pass away with a great noise, and the elements will melt with fervent heat; both the earth and the works that are in it will be burned up. Therefore, since all these things will be dissolved, what manner of persons ought you to be in holy conduct and godliness, looking for and hastening the coming of the day of God, because of which the heavens will be dissolved, being on fire, and the elements will melt with fervent heat?

2 PETER 3:10–12

Men of Galilee, why do you stand gazing up into heaven? This same Jesus, who was taken up from you into heaven, will so come in like manner as you saw Him go into heaven.

ACTS 1:11

He who believes in the Son of God has the witness in himself; he who does not believe God has made Him a liar, because he has not believed the testimony that God has given of His Son. And this is the testimony: that God has given us eternal life, and this life is in His Son. He who has the Son has life; he who does not have the Son of God does not have life. These things I have written to you who believe in the name of the Son of God, that you may know that you have eternal life, and that you may continue to believe in the name of the Son of God.

1 JOHN 5:10–13

And God will wipe away every tear from their eyes; there shall be no more death, nor sorrow, nor crying. There shall be no more pain, for the former things have passed away.

REVELATION 21:4

Looking for the blessed hope and glorious appearing of our great God and Savior Jesus Christ.

TITUS 2:13

Their descendants shall be known among
     the Gentiles,
And their offspring among the people.
All who see them shall acknowledge them,
That they are the posterity whom the
     LORD has blessed.
I will greatly rejoice in the LORD,
My soul shall be joyful in my God;
For He has clothed me with the garments
     of salvation,
He has covered me with the robe of
     righteousness,
As a bridegroom decks himself with
     ornaments,
And as a bride adorns herself with her jewels.
For as the earth brings forth its bud,
As the garden causes the things that are
     sown in it to spring forth,
So the Lord GOD will cause righteousness
     and praise to spring forth before all the
     nations.

ISAIAH 61:9–11

For I will pour water on him who is thirsty,
And floods on the dry ground;
I will pour My Spirit on your descendants,
And My blessing on your offspring.

ISAIAH 44:3

For as many of you as were baptized into Christ have put on Christ. There is neither Jew nor Greek, there is neither slave nor free, there is neither male nor female; for you are all one in Christ Jesus. And if you are Christ's, then you are Abraham's seed, and heirs according to the promise.

GALATIANS 3:27–29

I am the vine, you are the branches. He who abides in Me, and I in him, bears much fruit; for without Me you can do nothing. If anyone does not abide in Me, he is cast out as a branch and is withered; and they gather them and throw them into the fire, and they are burned. If you abide in Me, and My words abide in you, you will ask what you desire, and it shall be done for you. By this My Father is glorified, that you bear much fruit; so you will be My disciples.

JOHN 15:5–8

Most assuredly, I say to you, he who believes in Me, the works that I do he will do also; and greater works than these he will do, because I go to My Father. And whatever you ask in My name, that I will do, that the Father may be glorified in the Son. If you ask anything in My name, I will do it.

JOHN 14:12–14

You did not choose Me, but I chose you and appointed you that you should go and bear fruit, and that your fruit should remain, that whatever you ask the Father in My name He may give you. These things I command you, that you love one another.

JOHN 15:16–17

In that day you will ask Me nothing. Most assuredly, I say to you, whatever you ask the Father in My name He will give you. Until now you have asked nothing in My name. Ask, and you will receive, that your joy may be full.

JOHN 16:23–24

My soul, wait silently for God alone,
For my expectation is from Him.
He only is my rock and my salvation;
He is my defense;
I shall not be moved.
In God is my salvation and my glory;
The rock of my strength,
And my refuge, is in God.
Trust in Him at all times, you people;
Pour out your heart before Him;
God is a refuge for us.

PSALM 62:5–8

Let all those who hate Zion
Be put to shame and turned back.
Let them be as the grass on the housetops,
Which withers before it grows up,
With which the reaper does not fill his hand,
Nor he who binds sheaves, his arms.
Neither let those who pass by them say,
"The blessing of the LORD be upon you;
We bless you in the name of the LORD!"

PSALM 129:5–8

Every word of God is pure;
He is a shield to those who put their trust in
   Him.

PROVERBS 30:5

I am the LORD, and there is no other;
There is no God besides Me.
I will gird you, though you have not known
   Me,
That they may know from the rising of the
   sun to its setting
That there is none besides Me.
I am the LORD, and there is no other.

ISAIAH 45:5–6

The LORD your God in your midst,
The Mighty One, will save;
He will rejoice over you with gladness,
He will quiet you with His love,
He will rejoice over you with singing.

ZEPHANIAH 3:17

Do not be deceived, my beloved brethren. Every good gift and every perfect gift is from above, and comes down from the Father of lights, with whom there is no variation or shadow of turning.

JAMES 1:16–17

For assuredly, I say to you, till heaven and earth pass away, one jot or one tittle will by no means pass from the law till all is fulfilled. Whoever therefore breaks one of the least of these commandments, and teaches men so, shall be called least in the kingdom of heaven; but whoever does and teaches them, he shall be called great in the kingdom of heaven. For I say to you, that unless your righteousness exceeds the righteousness of the scribes and Pharisees, you will by no means enter the kingdom of heaven.

MATTHEW 5:18–20

I waited patiently for the LORD;
And He inclined to me,
And heard my cry.

PSALM 40:1

For He Himself is our peace, who has made both one, and has broken down the middle wall of separation, having abolished in His flesh the enmity, that is, the law of commandments contained in ordinances, so as to create in Himself one new man from the two, thus making peace, and that He might reconcile them both to God in one body through the cross, thereby putting to death the enmity. And He came and preached peace to you who were afar off and to those who were near. For through Him we both have access by one Spirit to the Father.

EPHESIANS 2:14–18

Moreover if your brother sins against you, go and tell him his fault between you and him alone. If he hears you, you have gained your brother.

MATTHEW 18:15

Where there is neither Greek nor Jew, circumcised nor uncircumcised, barbarian, Scythian, slave nor free, but Christ is all and in all.

COLOSSIANS 3:11

If someone says, "I love God," and hates his brother, he is a liar; for he who does not love his brother whom he has seen, how can he love God whom he has not seen?

1 JOHN 4:20

Jesus said to him, "You shall love the LORD your God with all your heart, with all your soul, and with all your mind. This is the first and great commandment. And the second is like it: You shall love your neighbor as yourself. On these two commandments hang all the Law and the Prophets."

MATTHEW 22:37–40

Behold, how good and how pleasant it is
For brethren to dwell together in unity!

PSALM 133:1

The glory which You gave Me I have given them, that they may be one just as We are one: "I in them, and You in Me; that they may be made perfect in one, and that the world may know that You have sent Me, and have loved them as You have loved Me."

JOHN 17:22–23

GOD'S ANSWERS FOR MEN

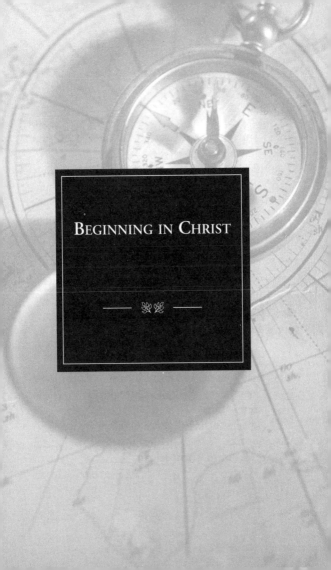

BEGINNING IN CHRIST

If you confess with your mouth the Lord Jesus and believe in your heart that God has raised Him from the dead, you will be saved.

For with the heart one believes unto righteousness, and with the mouth confession is made unto salvation.

For the Scripture says, "Whoever believes on Him will not be put to shame."

ROMANS 10:9–11

Most assuredly, I say to you, he who hears My word and believes in Him who sent Me has everlasting life, and shall not come into judgment, but has passed from death into life.

JOHN 5:24

You are all sons of God through faith in Christ Jesus.

For as many of you as were baptized into Christ have put on Christ.

There is neither Jew nor Greek, there is neither slave nor free, there is neither male nor female; for you are all one in Christ Jesus.

GALATIANS 3:26–28

If anyone is in Christ, he is a new creation; old things have passed away; behold, all things have become new.

2 CORINTHIANS 5:17

Whoever confesses Me before men, him I will also confess before My Father who is in heaven.

And he who does not take his cross and follow after Me is not worthy of Me.

He who finds his life will lose it, and he who loses his life for My sake will find it.

MATTHEW 10:32, 38–39

I have been crucified with Christ; it is no longer I who live, but Christ lives in me; and the life which I now live in the flesh I live by faith in the Son of God, who loved me and gave Himself for me.

GALATIANS 2:20

Having been born again, not of corruptible seed but incorruptible, through the word of God which lives and abides forever.

1 PETER 1:23

We know that we have passed from death to life, because we love the brethren. He who does not love his brother abides in death.

1 JOHN 3:14

Those who are Christ's have crucified the flesh with its passions and desires.

If we live in the Spirit, let us also walk in the Spirit.

GALATIANS 5:24–25

I will give you a new heart and put a new spirit within you; I will take the heart of stone out of your flesh and give you a heart of flesh.

I will put My Spirit within you and cause you to walk in My statutes, and you will keep My judgments and do them.

EZEKIEL 36:26–27

He who received seed on the good ground is he who hears the word and understands it, who indeed bears fruit and produces: some a hundredfold, some sixty, some thirty.

MATTHEW 13:23

Knowing this, that our old man was crucified with Him, that the body of sin might be done away with, that we should no longer be slaves of sin.

For he who has died has been freed from sin.

Now if we died with Christ, we believe that we shall also live with Him.

ROMANS 6:6–8

Looking unto Jesus, the author and finisher of our faith, who for the joy that was set before Him endured the cross, despising the shame, and has sat down at the right hand of the throne of God.

HEBREWS 12:2

Jesus said to them, "I am the bread of life. He who comes to Me shall never hunger, and he who believes in Me shall never thirst."

JOHN 6:35

Let your conduct be without covetousness; be content with such things as you have. For He Himself has said, "I will never leave you nor forsake you."

So we may boldly say: "The LORD is my helper; I will not fear. What can man do to me?"

Jesus Christ is the same yesterday, today, and forever.

HEBREWS 13:5–6, 8

If the Son makes you free, you shall be free indeed.

JOHN 8:36

I can do all things through Christ who strengthens me.

PHILIPPIANS 4:13

For in Him dwells all the fullness of the Godhead bodily; and you are complete in Him, who is the head of all principality and power.

COLOSSIANS 2:9–10

I am the good shepherd. The good shepherd gives His life for the sheep.

JOHN 10:11

> The LORD is my shepherd;
> I shall not want.
> He makes me to lie down in green pastures;
> He leads me beside the still waters.
> He restores my soul;
> He leads me in the paths of righteousness
> For His name's sake.
> Yea, though I walk through the valley of the
>   shadow of death,
> I will fear no evil;
> For You are with me;
> Your rod and Your staff, they comfort me.

PSALM 23:1–4

We have such trust through Christ toward God.

Not that we are sufficient of ourselves to think of anything as being from ourselves, but our sufficiency is from God.

2 Corinthians 3:4–5

The Lord stood with me and strengthened me, so that the message might be preached fully through me, and that all the Gentiles might hear. And I was delivered out of the mouth of the lion.

And the Lord will deliver me from every evil work and preserve me for His heavenly kingdom. To Him be glory forever and ever. Amen!

2 Timothy 4:17–18

My help comes from the Lord,
Who made heaven and earth.
He will not allow your foot to be moved;
He who keeps you will not slumber.

Psalm 121:2–3

Jesus said to him, "I am the way, the truth, and the life. No one comes to the Father except through Me."

John 14:6

This is My blood of the new covenant, which is shed for many for the remission of sins.

MATTHEW 26:28

Being justified freely by His grace through the redemption that is in Christ Jesus, whom God set forth as a propitiation by His blood, through faith, to demonstrate His righteousness, because in His forbearance God had passed over the sins that were previously committed, to demonstrate at the present time His righteousness, that He might be just and the justifier of the one who has faith in Jesus.

ROMANS 3:24–26

For the life of the flesh is in the blood, and I have given it to you upon the altar to make atonement for your souls; for it is the blood that makes atonement for the soul.

LEVITICUS 17:11

How much more shall the blood of Christ, who through the eternal Spirit offered Himself without spot to God, cleanse your conscience from dead works to serve the living God?

HEBREWS 9:14

God demonstrates His own love toward us, in that while we were still sinners, Christ died for us.

Much more then, having now been justified by His blood, we shall be saved from wrath through Him.

For if when we were enemies we were reconciled to God through the death of His Son, much more, having been reconciled, we shall be saved by His life.

ROMANS 5:8–10

If we walk in the light as He is in the light, we have fellowship with one another, and the blood of Jesus Christ His Son cleanses us from all sin.

1 JOHN 1:7

Then Jesus said to them, "Most assuredly, I say to you, unless you eat the flesh of the Son of Man and drink His blood, you have no life in you.

"Whoever eats My flesh and drinks My blood has eternal life, and I will raise him up at the last day.

"He who eats My flesh and drinks My blood abides in Me, and I in him."

JOHN 6:53, 54, 56

In Him we have redemption through His blood, the forgiveness of sins, according to the riches of His grace.

EPHESIANS 1:7

Then likewise he sprinkled with blood both the tabernacle and all the vessels of the ministry.

And according to the law almost all things are purified with blood, and without shedding of blood there is no remission.

HEBREWS 9:21–22

Knowing that you were not redeemed with corruptible things, like silver or gold, from your aimless conduct received by tradition from your fathers, but with the precious blood of Christ, as of a lamb without blemish and without spot.

He indeed was foreordained before the foundation of the world, but was manifest in these last times for you who through Him believe in God, who raised Him from the dead and gave Him glory, so that your faith and hope are in God.

1 PETER 1:18–21

How to Know the Power of God's Word

The word of God is living and powerful, and sharper than any two-edged sword, piercing even to the division of soul and spirit, and of joints and marrow, and is a discerner of the thoughts and intents of the heart.

HEBREWS 4:12

By the word of the LORD the heavens were made, and all the host of them by the breath of His mouth.

PSALM 33:6

Your word I have hidden in my heart, that I might not sin against You!

I will delight myself in Your statutes; I will not forget Your word.

PSALM 119:11, 16

How sweet are Your words to my taste,
Sweeter than honey to my mouth!
Through Your precepts I get understanding;
Therefore I hate every false way.
Your word is a lamp to my feet
And a light to my path.

PSALM 119:103–105

Forever, O Lord,
Your word is settled in heaven.
Your faithfulness endures to all generations;
You established the earth, and it abides.

PSALM 119:89–90

Your testimonies are wonderful;
Therefore my soul keeps them.
The entrance of Your words gives light;
It gives understanding to the simple.

PSALM 119:29–30

As newborn babes, desire the pure milk of the word,
that you may grow thereby, if indeed you have tasted
that the Lord is gracious.

1 PETER 2:2–3

You are already clean because of the word which I
have spoken to you.

JOHN 15:3

The grass withers, the flower fades, but the word of
our God stands forever.

ISAIAH 40:8

Heaven and earth will pass away, but My words will
by no means pass away.

LUKE 21:33

He answered and said, "It is written, 'Man shall not live by bread alone, but by every word that proceeds from the mouth of God.' "

MATTHEW 4:4

Having been born again, not of corruptible seed but incorruptible, through the word of God which lives and abides forever, because "All flesh is as grass, and all the glory of man as the flower of the grass. The grass withers, and its flower falls away, but the word of the LORD endures forever."

Now this is the word which by the gospel was preached to you.

1 PETER 1:23–25

It is the Spirit who gives life; the flesh profits nothing. The words that I speak to you are spirit, and they are life.

JOHN 6:63

Then Jesus said to those Jews who believed Him, "If you abide in My word, you are My disciples indeed.

"And you shall know the truth, and the truth shall make you free."

JOHN 8:31–32

And being assembled together with them, He commanded them not to depart from Jerusalem, but to wait for the Promise of the Father, "which," He said, "you have heard from Me; "for John truly baptized with water, but you shall be baptized with the Holy Spirit not many days from now."

Therefore, when they had come together, they asked Him, saying, "Lord, will You at this time restore the kingdom to Israel?"

And He said to them, "It is not for you to know times or seasons which the Father has put in His own authority.

"But you shall receive power when the Holy Spirit has come upon you; and you shall be witnesses to Me in Jerusalem, and in all Judea and Samaria, and to the end of the earth."

ACTS 1:4–8

See that you do not refuse Him who speaks. For if they did not escape who refused Him who spoke on earth, much more shall we not escape if we turn away from Him who speaks from heaven.

HEBREWS 12:25

But the fruit of the Spirit is love, joy, peace, longsuffering, kindness, goodness, faithfulness, gentleness, self-control. Against such there is no law.

And those who are Christ's have crucified the flesh with its passions and desires.

If we live in the Spirit, let us also walk in the Spirit.

GALATIANS 5:22–25

It is not you who speak, but the Spirit of your Father who speaks in you.

MATTHEW 10:20

So shall they fear
The name of the LORD from the west,
And His glory from the rising of the sun;
When the enemy comes in like a flood,
The Spirit of the LORD will lift up a standard
against him.

ISAIAH 59:19

The Holy Spirit will teach you in that very hour what you ought to say.

LUKE 12:12

Do not grieve the Holy Spirit of God, by whom you were sealed for the day of redemption.

EPHESIANS 4:30

Who also made us sufficient as ministers of the new covenant, not of the letter but of the Spirit; for the letter kills, but the Spirit gives life.

Now the Lord is the Spirit; and where the Spirit of the Lord is, there is liberty.

But we all, with unveiled face, beholding as in a mirror the glory of the Lord, are being transformed into the same image from glory to glory, just as by the Spirit of the Lord.

2 CORINTHIANS 3:6, 17–18

Knowing this first, that no prophecy of Scripture is of any private interpretation, for prophecy never came by the will of man, but holy men of God spoke as they were moved by the Holy Spirit.

2 PETER 1:20–21

But you, beloved, building yourselves up on your most holy faith, praying in the Holy Spirit, keep yourselves in the love of God, looking for the mercy of our Lord Jesus Christ unto eternal life.

JUDE 20, 21

Behold, I send the Promise of My Father upon you; but tarry in the city of Jerusalem until you are endued with power from on high.

LUKE 24:49

Abide in Me, and I in you. As the branch cannot bear fruit of itself, unless it abides in the vine, neither can you, unless you abide in Me.

I am the vine, you are the branches. He who abides in Me, and I in him, bears much fruit; for without Me you can do nothing.

If anyone does not abide in Me, he is cast out as a branch and is withered; and they gather them and throw them into the fire, and they are burned.

If you abide in Me, and My words abide in you, you will ask what you desire, and it shall be done for you.

JOHN 15:4–7

And now, little children, abide in Him, that when He appears, we may have confidence and not be ashamed before Him at His coming.

1 JOHN 2:28

I love those who love me, and those who seek me diligently will find me.

PROVERBS 8:17

I will meditate on Your precepts,
And contemplate Your ways.
I will delight myself in Your statutes;
I will not forget Your word.

PSALM 119:15–16

Let the word of Christ dwell in you richly in all wisdom, teaching and admonishing one another in psalms and hymns and spiritual songs, singing with grace in your hearts to the Lord.

COLOSSIANS 3:16

Those who wait on the LORD
Shall renew their strength;
They shall mount up with wings like eagles,
They shall run and not be weary,
They shall walk and not faint.

ISAIAH 40:31

Draw near to God and He will draw near to you. Cleanse your hands, you sinners; and purify your hearts, you double-minded.

JAMES 4:8

But put on the Lord Jesus Christ, and make no provision for the flesh, to fulfill its lusts.

ROMANS 13:14

Now by this we know that we know Him, if we keep His commandments.

He who says, "I know Him," and does not keep His commandments, is a liar, and the truth is not in him.

But whoever keeps His word, truly the love of God is perfected in him. By this we know that we are in Him.

He who says he abides in Him ought himself also to walk just as He walked.

1 JOHN 2:3–6

In Him we live and move and have our being, as also some of your own poets have said, "For we are also His offspring."

ACTS 17:28

Blessed is the man who listens to me,
Watching daily at my gates,
Waiting at the posts of my doors.

PROVERBS 8:34

As newborn babes, desire the pure milk of the word, that you may grow thereby.

1 PETER 2:2

But be doers of the word, and not hearers only, deceiving yourselves.

JAMES 1:22

Now faith is the substance of things hoped for, the evidence of things not seen.

By faith we understand that the worlds were framed by the word of God, so that the things which are seen were not made of things which are visible.

But without faith it is impossible to please Him, for he who comes to God must believe that He is, and that He is a rewarder of those who diligently seek Him.

By faith he forsook Egypt, not fearing the wrath of the king; for he endured as seeing Him who is invisible.

HEBREWS 11:1, 3, 6, 27

That the genuineness of your faith, being much more precious than gold that perishes, though it is tested by fire, may be found to praise, honor, and glory at the revelation of Jesus Christ, whom having not seen you love. Though now you do not see Him, yet believing, you rejoice with joy inexpressible and full of glory, receiving the end of your faith—the salvation of your souls.

1 PETER 1:7–9

For with God nothing will be impossible.

LUKE 1:37

For in it the righteousness of God is revealed from faith to faith; as it is written, "The just shall live by faith."

ROMANS 1:17

So then faith comes by hearing, and hearing by the word of God.

ROMANS 10:17

Have I not commanded you? Be strong and of good courage; do not be afraid, nor be dismayed, for the LORD your God is with you wherever you go.

JOSHUA 1:9

If any of you lacks wisdom, let him ask of God, who gives to all liberally and without reproach, and it will be given to him.

But let him ask in faith, with no doubting, for he who doubts is like a wave of the sea driven and tossed by the wind.

For let not that man suppose that he will receive anything from the Lord; he is a double-minded man, unstable in all his ways.

JAMES 1:5–8

He did not waver at the promise of God through unbelief, but was strengthened in faith, giving glory to God, and being fully convinced that what He had promised He was also able to perform.

ROMANS 4:20–21

We are hard pressed on every side, yet not crushed; we are perplexed, but not in despair; persecuted, but not forsaken; struck down, but not destroyed—always carrying about in the body the dying of the Lord Jesus, that the life of Jesus also may be manifested in our body.

2 CORINTHIANS 4:8–10

What then shall we say to these things? If God is for us, who can be against us?

ROMANS 8:31

But you, beloved, building yourselves up on your most holy faith, praying in the Holy Spirit, keep yourselves in the love of God, looking for the mercy of our Lord Jesus Christ unto eternal life.

JUDE 20, 21

We walk by faith, not by sight.

2 CORINTHIANS 5:7

GROWING IN CHRIST

———— ❀❀ ————

For you, brethren, have been called to liberty; only do not use liberty as an opportunity for the flesh, but through love serve one another.

For all the law is fulfilled in one word, even in this: "You shall love your neighbor as yourself."

But if you bite and devour one another, beware lest you be consumed by one another!

I say then: Walk in the Spirit, and you shall not fulfill the lust of the flesh.

For the flesh lusts against the Spirit, and the Spirit against the flesh; and these are contrary to one another, so that you do not do the things that you wish.

GALATIANS 5:13–17

I beseech you therefore, brethren, by the mercies of God, that you present your bodies a living sacrifice, holy, acceptable to God, which is your reasonable service.

And do not be conformed to this world, but be transformed by the renewing of your mind, that you may prove what is that good and acceptable and perfect will of God.

ROMANS 12:1–2

For the law of the Spirit of life in Christ Jesus has made me free from the law of sin and death.

For what the law could not do in that it was weak through the flesh, God did by sending His own Son in the likeness of sinful flesh, on account of sin: He condemned sin in the flesh, that the righteous requirement of the law might be fulfilled in us who do not walk according to the flesh but according to the Spirit.

For those who live according to the flesh set their minds on the things of the flesh, but those who live according to the Spirit, the things of the Spirit.

For to be carnally minded is death, but to be spiritually minded is life and peace.

Because the carnal mind is enmity against God; for it is not subject to the law of God, nor indeed can be.

So then, those who are in the flesh cannot please God.

But you are not in the flesh but in the Spirit, if indeed the Spirit of God dwells in you. Now if anyone does not have the Spirit of Christ, he is not His.

And if Christ is in you, the body is dead because of sin, but the Spirit is life because of righteousness.

But if the Spirit of Him who raised Jesus from the dead dwells in you, He who raised Christ from the dead will also give life to your mortal bodies through His Spirit who dwells in you.

ROMANS 8:2–11

Who has known the mind of the LORD that he may instruct Him? But we have the mind of Christ.

1 CORINTHIANS 2:16

Therefore gird up the loins of your mind, be sober, and rest your hope fully upon the grace that is to be brought to you at the revelation of Jesus Christ; as obedient children, not conforming yourselves to the former lusts, as in your ignorance; but as He who called you is holy, you also be holy in all your conduct.

1 PETER 1:13–15

I have been crucified with Christ; it is no longer I who live, but Christ lives in me; and the life which I now live in the flesh I live by faith in the Son of God, who loved me and gave Himself for me.

GALATIANS 2:20

Beware lest anyone cheat you through philosophy and empty deceit, according to the tradition of men, according to the basic principles of the world, and not according to Christ.

COLOSSIANS 2:8

Therefore we do not lose heart. Even though our outward man is perishing, yet the inward man is being renewed day by day.

2 CORINTHIANS 4:16

Finally, my brethren, be strong in the Lord and in the power of His might.

Put on the whole armor of God, that you may be able to stand against the wiles of the devil.

For we do not wrestle against flesh and blood, but against principalities, against powers, against the rulers of the darkness of this age, against spiritual hosts of wickedness in the heavenly places.

Therefore take up the whole armor of God, that you may be able to withstand in the evil day, and having done all, to stand.

Stand therefore, having girded your waist with truth, having put on the breastplate of righteousness, and having shod your feet with the preparation of the gospel of peace; above all, taking the shield of faith with which you will be able to quench all the fiery darts of the wicked one.

And take the helmet of salvation, and the sword of the Spirit, which is the word of God.

EPHESIANS 6:10–17

In that He Himself has suffered, being tempted, He is able to aid those who are tempted.

HEBREWS 2:18

Submit to God. Resist the devil and he will flee from you.

Draw near to God and He will draw near to you. Cleanse your hands, you sinners; and purify your hearts, you double-minded.

JAMES 4:7–8

And He said to them, "I saw Satan fall like lightning from heaven. Behold, I give you the authority to trample on serpents and scorpions, and over all the power of the enemy, and nothing shall by any means hurt you."

LUKE 10:18–19

He who sins is of the devil, for the devil has sinned from the beginning. For this purpose the Son of God was manifested, that He might destroy the works of the devil.

1 JOHN 3:8

The LORD shall preserve you from all evil;
He shall preserve your soul.
The LORD shall preserve your going out and
    your coming in
From this time forth, and even forevermore.

PSALM 121:7–8

Be sober, be vigilant; because your adversary the devil walks about like a roaring lion, seeking whom he may devour.

Resist him, steadfast in the faith, knowing that the same sufferings are experienced by your brotherhood in the world.

But may the God of all grace, who called us to His eternal glory by Christ Jesus, after you have suffered a while, perfect, establish, strengthen, and settle you.

1 PETER 5:8–10

Surely He shall deliver you from the snare of
    the fowler
And from the perilous pestilence.
He shall cover you with His feathers,
And under His wings you shall take refuge;
His truth shall be your shield and buckler.
You shall not be afraid of the terror by night,
Nor of the arrow that flies by day,
Nor of the pestilence that walks in darkness,
Nor of the destruction that lays waste at
    noonday.
A thousand may fall at your side,
And ten thousand at your right hand;
But it shall not come near you.

PSALM 91:3–7

Beware of false prophets, who come to you in sheep's clothing, but inwardly they are ravenous wolves.

You will know them by their fruits. Do men gather grapes from thornbushes or figs from thistles?

Even so, every good tree bears good fruit, but a bad tree bears bad fruit.

Therefore by their fruits you will know them.

Not everyone who says to Me, "Lord, Lord," shall enter the kingdom of heaven, but he who does the will of My Father in heaven.

Many will say to Me in that day, "Lord, Lord, have we not prophesied in Your name, cast out demons in Your name, and done many wonders in Your name?"

And then I will declare to them, "I never knew you; depart from Me, you who practice lawlessness!"

MATTHEW 7:15–17, 20–23

They profess to know God, but in works they deny Him, being abominable, disobedient, and disqualified for every good work.

TITUS 1:16

Beloved, do not believe every spirit, but test the spirits, whether they are of God; because many false prophets have gone out into the world.

By this you know the Spirit of God: Every spirit that confesses that Jesus Christ has come in the flesh is of God, and every spirit that does not confess that Jesus Christ has come in the flesh is not of God. And this is the spirit of the Antichrist, which you have heard was coming, and is now already in the world.

1 JOHN 4:1–3

And when they say to you, "Seek those who are mediums and wizards, who whisper and mutter," should not a people seek their God? Should they seek the dead on behalf of the living?

To the law and to the testimony! If they do not speak according to this word, it is because there is no light in them.

ISAIAH 8:19–20

Stand fast therefore in the liberty by which Christ has made us free, and do not be entangled again with a yoke of bondage.

GALATIANS 5:1

"Behold, I am against those who prophesy false dreams," says the LORD, "and tell them, and cause My people to err by their lies and by their recklessness. Yet I did not send them or command them; therefore they shall not profit this people at all," says the LORD.

JEREMIAH 23:32

A good tree does not bear bad fruit, nor does a bad tree bear good fruit.

For every tree is known by its own fruit. For men do not gather figs from thorns, nor do they gather grapes from a bramble bush.

LUKE 6:43–44

For God is not the author of confusion but of peace, as in all the churches of the saints.

1 CORINTHIANS 14:33

God has not given us a spirit of fear, but of power and of love and of a sound mind.

2 TIMOTHY 1:7

He who sins is of the devil, for the devil has sinned from the beginning. For this purpose the Son of God was manifested, that He might destroy the works of the devil.

1 JOHN 3:8

No one can serve two masters; for either he will hate the one and love the other, or else he will be loyal to the one and despise the other. You cannot serve God and mammon.

MATTHEW 6:24

Do not love the world or the things in the world. If anyone loves the world, the love of the Father is not in him.

For all that is in the world—the lust of the flesh, the lust of the eyes, and the pride of life—is not of the Father but is of the world.

And the world is passing away, and the lust of it; but he who does the will of God abides forever.

1 JOHN 2:15–17

Do not be conformed to this world, but be transformed by the renewing of your mind, that you may prove what is that good and acceptable and perfect will of God.

ROMANS 12:2

Have no fellowship with the unfruitful works of darkness, but rather expose them.

EPHESIANS 5:11

And do this, knowing the time, that now it is high time to awake out of sleep; for now our salvation is nearer than when we first believed.

The night is far spent, the day is at hand. Therefore let us cast off the works of darkness, and let us put on the armor of light.

Let us walk properly, as in the day, not in revelry and drunkenness, not in lewdness and lust, not in strife and envy.

But put on the Lord Jesus Christ, and make no provision for the flesh, to fulfill its lusts.

ROMANS 13:11–14

The Lord knows how to deliver the godly out of temptations and to reserve the unjust under punishment for the day of judgment.

2 PETER 2:9

Then He said to them all, "If anyone desires to come after Me, let him deny himself, and take up his cross daily, and follow Me.

"For whoever desires to save his life will lose it, but whoever loses his life for My sake will save it.

"For what profit is it to a man if he gains the whole world, and is himself destroyed or lost?"

LUKE 9:23–25

Now therefore, fear the LORD, serve Him in sincerity and in truth, and put away the gods which your fathers served on the other side of the River and in Egypt. Serve the LORD!

JOSHUA 24:14

Choosing rather to suffer affliction with the people of God than to enjoy the passing pleasures of sin, esteeming the reproach of Christ greater riches than the treasures in Egypt; for he looked to the reward.

By faith he forsook Egypt, not fearing the wrath of the king; for he endured as seeing Him who is invisible.

HEBREWS 11:25–27

By which have been given to us exceedingly great and precious promises, that through these you may be partakers of the divine nature, having escaped the corruption that is in the world through lust.

2 PETER 1:4

Take heed to yourselves, lest your hearts be weighed down with carousing, drunkenness, and cares of this life, and that Day come on you unexpectedly.

LUKE 21:34

Do you not know that your bodies are members of Christ? Shall I then take the members of Christ and make them members of a harlot? Certainly not!

Or do you not know that he who is joined to a harlot is one body with her? For "the two," He says, "shall become one flesh."

But he who is joined to the Lord is one spirit with Him.

Flee sexual immorality. Every sin that a man does is outside the body, but he who commits sexual immorality sins against his own body.

Or do you not know that your body is the temple of the Holy Spirit who is in you, whom you have from God, and you are not your own?

For you were bought at a price; therefore glorify God in your body and in your spirit, which are God's.

1 CORINTHIANS 6:15–20

I say then: Walk in the Spirit, and you shall not fulfill the lust of the flesh.

For the flesh lusts against the Spirit, and the Spirit against the flesh; and these are contrary to one another, so that you do not do the things that you wish.

GALATIANS 5:16–17

No temptation has overtaken you except such as is common to man; but God is faithful, who will not allow you to be tempted beyond what you are able, but with the temptation will also make the way of escape, that you may be able to bear it.

1 CORINTHIANS 10:13

Put off, concerning your former conduct, the old man which grows corrupt according to the deceitful lusts, and be renewed in the spirit of your mind, and . . . put on the new man which was created according to God, in true righteousness and holiness . . . nor give place to the devil.

EPHESIANS 4:22–24, 27

Now therefore, listen to me, my children;
Pay attention to the words of my mouth:
Do not let your heart turn aside to her ways,
Do not stray into her paths;
For she has cast down many wounded,
And all who were slain by her were strong
     men.
Her house is the way to hell,
Descending to the chambers of death.

PROVERBS 7:24–27

The Lord knows how to deliver the godly out of temptations and to reserve the unjust under punishment for the day of judgment.

2 PETER 2:9

My brethren, count it all joy when you fall into various trials, knowing that the testing of your faith produces patience.

But let patience have its perfect work, that you may be perfect and complete, lacking nothing.

JAMES 1:2–4

Do not lust after her beauty in your heart,
Nor let her allure you with her eyelids.
For by means of a harlot
A man is reduced to a crust of bread;
And an adulteress will prey upon his precious life.

PROVERBS 6:25–26

Now therefore, listen to me, my children;
Pay attention to the words of my mouth:
Do not let your heart turn aside to her ways,
Do not stray into her paths;
For she has cast down many wounded,
And all who were slain by her were strong men.
Her house is the way to hell,
Descending to the chambers of death.

PROVERBS 7:24–27

Pride goes before destruction,
And a haughty spirit before a fall.
Better to be of a humble spirit with the lowly,
Than to divide the spoil with the proud.
He who heeds the word wisely will find good,
And whoever trusts in the LORD, happy is he.

PROVERBS 16:18–20

He who is of a proud heart stirs up strife,
But he who trusts in the LORD will be prospered.
He who trusts in his own heart is a fool,
But whoever walks wisely will be delivered.

PROVERBS 28:25–26

Then Jesus called a little child to Him, set him in the midst of them, and said, "Assuredly, I say to you, unless you are converted and become as little children, you will by no means enter the kingdom of heaven. Therefore whoever humbles himself as this little child is the greatest in the kingdom of heaven."

MATTHEW 18:2–4

But He gives more grace. Therefore He says: "God resists the proud, but gives grace to the humble."

Therefore submit to God. Resist the devil and he will flee from you.

Humble yourselves in the sight of the Lord, and He will lift you up.

JAMES 4:6–7, 10

Yet it shall not be so among you; but whoever desires to become great among you, let him be your servant

And whoever desires to be first among you, let him be your slave.

MATTHEW 20:26–27

Likewise you younger people, submit yourselves to your elders. Yes, all of you be submissive to one another, and be clothed with humility, for "God resists the proud, but gives grace to the humble."

Therefore humble yourselves under the mighty hand of God, that He may exalt you in due time.

1 PETER 5:5–6

But we have this treasure in earthen vessels, that the excellence of the power may be of God and not of us.

2 CORINTHIANS 4:7

Hear and give ear:
Do not be proud,
For the LORD has spoken.
Give glory to the LORD your God
Before He causes darkness,
And before your feet stumble
On the dark mountains,
And while you are looking for light,
He turns it into the shadow of death
And makes it dense darkness.
But if you will not hear it,
My soul will weep in secret for your pride;
My eyes will weep bitterly
And run down with tears,
Because the LORD's flock has been taken
        captive.

JEREMIAH 13:15-17

Take My yoke upon you and learn from Me, for I am gentle and lowly in heart, and you will find rest for your souls.

For My yoke is easy and My burden is light.

MATTHEW 11:29–30

The fear of the LORD is the instruction of wisdom, and before honor is humility.

PROVERBS 15:33

Death and life are in the power of the tongue, and those who love it will eat its fruit.

PROVERBS 18:21

Let no corrupt word proceed out of your mouth, but what is good for necessary edification, that it may impart grace to the hearers.

Let all bitterness, wrath, anger, clamor, and evil speaking be put away from you, with all malice.

And be kind to one another, tenderhearted, forgiving one another, just as God in Christ forgave you.

EPHESIANS 4:29, 31–32

Pleasant words are like a honeycomb, Sweetness to the soul and health to the bones.

PROVERBS 16:24

He who guards his mouth preserves his life, But he who opens wide his lips shall have destruction.

PROVERBS 13:3

A good man out of the good treasure of his heart brings forth good; and an evil man out of the evil treasure of his heart brings forth evil. For out of the abundance of the heart his mouth speaks.

LUKE 6:45

But I say to you that for every idle word men may speak, they will give account of it in the day of judgment.

MATTHEW 12:36

Sing to Him, sing psalms to Him; talk of all His wondrous works!

1 CHRONICLES 16:9

Whoever guards his mouth and tongue keeps his soul from troubles.

PROVERBS 21:23

Do not be a witness against your neighbor without cause, for would you deceive with your lips?

PROVERBS 24:28

Avoid foolish disputes, genealogies, contentions, and strivings about the law; for they are unprofitable and useless.

TITUS 3:9

O Timothy! Guard what was committed to your trust, avoiding the profane and idle babblings and contradictions of what is falsely called knowledge— by professing it some have strayed concerning the faith. Grace be with you. Amen.

1 TIMOTHY 6:20–21

As long as my breath is in me,
And the breath of God in my nostrils,
My lips will not speak wickedness,
Nor my tongue utter deceit.

JOB 27:3–4

As He who called you is holy, you also be holy in all your conduct.

1 PETER 1:15

Who, when He was reviled, did not revile in return; when He suffered, He did not threaten, but committed Himself to Him who judges righteously.

1 PETER 2:23

He who would love life and see good days, let him refrain his tongue from evil, and his lips from speaking deceit.

1 PETER 3:10

Let the word of Christ dwell in you richly in all wisdom, teaching and admonishing one another in psalms and hymns and spiritual songs, singing with grace in your hearts to the Lord.

And whatever you do in word or deed, do all in the name of the Lord Jesus, giving thanks to God the Father through Him.

COLOSSIANS 3:16–17

I love those who love me, and those who seek me diligently will find me.

PROVERBS 8:17

Seek the LORD and His strength;
Seek His face evermore!
Remember His marvelous works which He
has done,
His wonders, and the judgments of His mouth,
1 CHRONICLES 16:11–12

Trust in Him at all times, you people; pour out your heart before Him; God is a refuge for us.

PSALM 62:8

You are My friends if you do whatever I command you.

No longer do I call you servants, for a servant does not know what his master is doing; but I have called you friends, for all things that I heard from My Father I have made known to you.

You did not choose Me, but I chose you and appointed you that you should go and bear fruit, and that your fruit should remain, that whatever you ask the Father in My name He may give you.

JOHN 15:14–16

Speaking to one another in psalms and hymns and spiritual songs, singing and making melody in your heart to the Lord, giving thanks always for all things to God the Father in the name of our Lord Jesus Christ.

EPHESIANS 5:19–20

I will bless the LORD at all times;
His praise shall continually be in my mouth.
My soul shall make its boast in the LORD;
The humble shall hear of it and be glad.
Oh, magnify the LORD with me,
And let us exalt His name together.
I sought the LORD, and He heard me,
And delivered me from all my fears.

PSALM 34:1–4

Truly my soul silently waits for God;
From Him comes my salvation.
He only is my rock and my salvation;
He is my defense;
I shall not be greatly moved.
My soul, wait silently for God alone,
For my expectation is from Him.
He only is my rock and my salvation;
He is my defense;
I shall not be moved.
In God is my salvation and my glory;
The rock of my strength,
And my refuge, is in God.

PSALM 62:1–2, 5–7

Put on the Lord Jesus Christ, and make no provision
for the flesh, to fulfill its lusts.

ROMANS 13:14

In You, O LORD, I put my trust;
Let me never be put to shame.
For You are my hope, O Lord GOD;
You are my trust from my youth.
Let my mouth be filled with Your praise
And with Your glory all the day.

PSALM 71:1, 5, 8

There is therefore now no condemnation to those who are in Christ Jesus, who do not walk according to the flesh, but according to the Spirit.

For the law of the Spirit of life in Christ Jesus has made me free from the law of sin and death.

ROMANS 8:1–2

For you, brethren, have been called to liberty; only do not use liberty as an opportunity for the flesh, but through love serve one another.

GALATIANS 5:13

There is neither Jew nor Greek, there is neither slave nor free, there is neither male nor female; for you are all one in Christ Jesus.

GALATIANS 3:28

But he who looks into the perfect law of liberty and continues in it, and is not a forgetful hearer but a doer of the work, this one will be blessed in what he does.

JAMES 1:25

Now the Lord is the Spirit; and where the Spirit of the Lord is, there is liberty.

2 CORINTHIANS 3:17

I, Jesus, have sent My angel to testify to you these things in the churches. I am the Root and the Offspring of David, the Bright and Morning Star.

And the Spirit and the bride say, "Come!" And let him who hears say, "Come!" And let him who thirsts come. Whoever desires, let him take the water of life freely.

REVELATION 22:16–17

"And you shall know the truth, and the truth shall make you free."

They answered Him, "We are Abraham's descendants, and have never been in bondage to anyone. How can you say, 'You will be made free'?"

Jesus answered them, "Most assuredly, I say to you, whoever commits sin is a slave of sin.

"And a slave does not abide in the house forever, but a son abides forever.

"Therefore if the Son makes you free, you shall be free indeed."

JOHN 8:32–36

Stand fast therefore in the liberty by which Christ has made us free, and do not be entangled again with a yoke of bondage.

GALATIANS 5:1

Am I not an apostle? Am I not free? Have I not seen Jesus Christ our Lord? Are you not my work in the Lord?

1 CORINTHIANS 9:1

And you shall know the truth, and the truth shall make you free.

Therefore if the Son makes you free, you shall be free indeed.

JOHN 8:32, 36

Now the Lord is the Spirit; and where the Spirit of the Lord is, there is liberty.

2 CORINTHIANS 3:17

Because the creation itself also will be delivered from the bondage of corruption into the glorious liberty of the children of God.

ROMANS 8:21

How to Praise the Lord

Because Your lovingkindness is better than
    life,
My lips shall praise You.
Thus I will bless You while I live;
I will lift up my hands in Your name.
My soul shall be satisfied as with marrow and
    fatness,
And my mouth shall praise You with joyful
    lips.

PSALM 63:3–5

I will bless the LORD at all times; His praise shall continually be in my mouth.

PSALM 34:1

Accept, I pray, the freewill offerings of my mouth, O LORD, and teach me Your judgments.

PSALM 119:108

At midnight Paul and Silas were praying and singing hymns to God, and the prisoners were listening to them.

ACTS 16:25

Praise the LORD!
Sing to the LORD a new song,
And His praise in the assembly of saints.
Let Israel rejoice in their Maker;
Let the children of Zion be joyful in their
     King.
Let them praise His name with the dance;
Let them sing praises to Him with the timbrel
   and harp.
For the LORD takes pleasure in His people;
He will beautify the humble with salvation.
Let the saints be joyful in glory;
Let them sing aloud on their beds.
Let the high praises of God be in their mouth,
And a two-edged sword in their hand,

PSALM 149:1–6

Whoever offers praise glorifies Me; and to him who orders his conduct aright I will show the salvation of God.

PSALM 50:23

Praise the LORD!
Praise God in His sanctuary;
Praise Him in His mighty firmament!
Praise Him for His mighty acts;
Praise Him according to His excellent great-
      ness!
Praise Him with the sound of the trumpet;
Praise Him with the lute and harp!
Praise Him with the timbrel and dance;
Praise Him with stringed instruments and
      flutes!
Praise Him with loud cymbals;
Praise Him with clashing cymbals!
Let everything that has breath praise the
      LORD.
Praise the LORD!

PSALM 150:1–6

Praise the LORD!
Praise, O servants of the LORD,
Praise the name of the LORD!
Blessed be the name of the LORD
From this time forth and forevermore!
From the rising of the sun to its going down
The LORD's name is to be praised.

PSALM 113:1–3

"The voice of joy and the voice of gladness, the voice of the bridegroom and the voice of the bride, the voice of those who will say: 'Praise the LORD of hosts, for the LORD is good, for His mercy endures forever'—and of those who will bring the sacrifice of praise into the house of the LORD. For I will cause the captives of the land to return as at the first," says the LORD.

JEREMIAH 33:11

You are a chosen generation, a royal priesthood, a holy nation, His own special people, that you may proclaim the praises of Him who called you out of darkness into His marvelous light.

1 PETER 2:9

His lord said to him, "Well done, good and faithful servant; you were faithful over a few things, I will make you ruler over many things. Enter into the joy of your lord."

MATTHEW 25:21

These things I have spoken to you, that My joy may remain in you, and that your joy may be full.

This is My commandment, that you love one another as I have loved you.

JOHN 15:11–12

Let all those rejoice who put their trust in
    You;
Let them ever shout for joy, because You
    defend them;
Let those also who love Your name
Be joyful in You.
For You, O LORD, will bless the righteous;
With favor You will surround him as with a
    shield.

PSALM 5:11–12

A merry heart makes a cheerful countenance, but by sorrow of the heart the spirit is broken.

PROVERBS 15:13

God has not given us a spirit of fear, but of power and of love and of a sound mind.

2 TIMOTHY 1:7

The kingdom of God is not eating and drinking, but righteousness and peace and joy in the Holy Spirit.

For he who serves Christ in these things is acceptable to God and approved by men.

ROMANS 14:17–18

"Nevertheless do not rejoice in this, that the spirits are subject to you, but rather rejoice because your names are written in heaven."

In that hour Jesus rejoiced in the Spirit and said, "I thank You, Father, Lord of heaven and earth, that You have hidden these things from the wise and prudent and revealed them to babes. Even so, Father, for so it seemed good in Your sight."

LUKE 10:20–21

A merry heart does good, like medicine, but a broken spirit dries the bones.

PROVERBS 17:22

You love righteousness and hate wickedness;
Therefore God, Your God, has anointed You
With the oil of gladness more than Your com-
        panions.
All Your garments are scented with myrrh and
        aloes and cassia,
Out of the ivory palaces, by which they have
        made You glad.

PSALM 45:7–8

And you became followers of us and of the Lord, having received the word in much affliction, with joy of
the Holy Spirit.

1 THESSALONIANS 1:6

Restore to me the joy of Your salvation,
And uphold me by Your generous Spirit.
Then I will teach transgressors Your ways,
And sinners shall be converted to You.

PSALM 51:12–13

This is the day the LORD has made;
        we will rejoice and be glad in it.

PSALM 118:24

MATURING IN CHRIST

❧❧

Beloved, do not think it strange concerning the fiery trial which is to try you, as though some strange thing happened to you; but rejoice to the extent that you partake of Christ's sufferings, that when His glory is revealed, you may also be glad with exceeding joy.

Yet if anyone suffers as a Christian, let him not be ashamed, but let him glorify God in this matter.

1 PETER 4:12–13, 16

When you pass through the waters, I will be
    with you;
And through the rivers, they shall not over-
    flow you.
When you walk through the fire, you shall
    not be burned,
Nor shall the flame scorch you.
For I am the LORD your God,
The Holy One of Israel, your Savior;
I gave Egypt for your ransom,
Ethiopia and Seba in your place.

ISAIAH 43:2–3

But He knows the way that I take;
When He has tested me, I shall come forth as
      gold.
My foot has held fast to His steps;
I have kept His way and not turned aside.

JOB 23:10–11

The righteous cry out, and the LORD hears,
And delivers them out of all their troubles.
The LORD is near to those who have a broken
      heart,
And saves such as have a contrite spirit.
Many are the afflictions of the righteous,
But the LORD delivers him out of them all.

PSALM 34:17–19

For You will light my lamp;
The LORD my God will enlighten my darkness.
For by You I can run against a troop,
By my God I can leap over a wall.
As for God, His way is perfect;
The word of the LORD is proven;
He is a shield to all who trust in Him.
It is God who arms me with strength,
And makes my way perfect.

PSALM 18:28–30, 32

Blessed is the man who endures temptation; for when he has been approved, he will receive the crown of life which the Lord has promised to those who love Him.

JAMES 1:12

Though He slay me, yet will I trust Him.
Even so, I will defend my own ways before Him.
He also shall be my salvation,
For a hypocrite could not come before Him.

JOB 13:15–16

Deliver me out of the mire,
And let me not sink;
Let me be delivered from those who hate me,
And out of the deep waters.
Let not the floodwater overflow me,
Nor let the deep swallow me up;
And let not the pit shut its mouth on me.
Hear me, O LORD, for Your lovingkindness is
     good;
Turn to me according to the multitude of
     Your tender mercies.
And do not hide Your face from Your servant,
For I am in trouble;
Hear me speedily.
Draw near to my soul, and redeem it;
Deliver me because of my enemies.

PSALM 69:14–18

Is anyone among you sick? Let him call for the elders of the church, and let them pray over him, anointing him with oil in the name of the Lord.

And the prayer of faith will save the sick, and the Lord will raise him up. And if he has committed sins, he will be forgiven.

JAMES 5:14–15

You will keep him in perfect peace,
Whose mind is stayed on You,
Because he trusts in You.
Trust in the LORD forever,
For in YAH, the LORD, is everlasting strength.

ISAIAH 26:3–4

Heal me, O LORD, and I shall be healed; save me, and I shall be saved, for You are my praise.

JEREMIAH 17:14

Who Himself bore our sins in His own body on the tree, that we, having died to sins, might live for righteousness—by whose stripes you were healed.

1 PETER 2:24

And I said, "This is my anguish;
But I will remember the years of the right
     hand of the Most High."
I will remember the works of the LORD;
Surely I will remember Your wonders of old.
I will also meditate on all Your work,
And talk of Your deeds.
Your way, O God, is in the sanctuary;
Who is so great a God as our God?
You are the God who does wonders;
You have declared Your strength among the
     peoples.

PSALM 77:10-14

Yea, though I walk through the valley of the shadow of death, I will fear no evil; for You are with me; Your rod and Your staff, they comfort me.

PSALM 23:4

For we know that if our earthly house, this tent, is destroyed, we have a building from God, a house not made with hands, eternal in the heavens.

2 CORINTHIANS 5:1

For this is God, our God forever and ever; He will be our guide even to death.

PSALM 48:14

But God will redeem my soul from the power of the grave, for He shall receive me.

PSALM 49:15

For all things are for your sakes, that grace, having spread through the many, may cause thanksgiving to abound to the glory of God.

Therefore we do not lose heart. Even though our outward man is perishing, yet the inward man is being renewed day by day.

For our light affliction, which is but for a moment, is working for us a far more exceeding and eternal weight of glory, while we do not look at the things which are seen, but at the things which are not seen. For the things which are seen are temporary, but the things which are not seen are eternal.

2 CORINTHIANS 4:15–18

I call to remembrance my song in the night; I meditate within my heart, and my spirit makes diligent search.

PSALM 77:6

Therefore, since Christ suffered for us in the flesh, arm yourselves also with the same mind, for he who has suffered in the flesh has ceased from sin, that he no longer should live the rest of his time in the flesh for the lusts of men, but for the will of God.

Beloved, do not think it strange concerning the fiery trial which is to try you, as though some strange thing happened to you; but rejoice to the extent that you partake of Christ's sufferings, that when His glory is revealed, you may also be glad with exceeding joy.

If you are reproached for the name of Christ, blessed are you, for the Spirit of glory and of God rests upon you. On their part He is blasphemed, but on your part He is glorified.

But let none of you suffer as a murderer, a thief, an evildoer, or as a busybody in other people's matters.

Yet if anyone suffers as a Christian, let him not be ashamed, but let him glorify God in this matter.

For the time has come for judgment to begin at the house of God; and if it begins with us first, what will be the end of those who do not obey the gospel of God?

1 Peter 4:1–2, 12–17

You therefore must endure hardship as a good soldier of Jesus Christ.

2 TIMOTHY 2:3

For whom the LORD loves He chastens, and scourges every son whom He receives.

If you endure chastening, God deals with you as with sons; for what son is there whom a father does not chasten?

But if you are without chastening, of which all have become partakers, then you are illegitimate and not sons.

Now no chastening seems to be joyful for the present, but painful; nevertheless, afterward it yields the peaceable fruit of righteousness to those who have been trained by it.

Therefore strengthen the hands which hang down, and the feeble knees, and make straight paths for your feet, so that what is lame may not be dislocated, but rather be healed.

HEBREWS 12:6–8,11–13

Blessed is the man who endures temptation; for when he has been approved, he will receive the crown of life which the Lord has promised to those who love Him.

JAMES 1:12

For what credit is it if, when you are beaten for your faults, you take it patiently? But when you do good and suffer, if you take it patiently, this is commendable before God.

For to this you were called, because Christ also suffered for us, leaving us an example, that you should follow His steps.

1 PETER 2:20–21

We see Jesus, who was made a little lower than the angels, for the suffering of death crowned with glory and honor, that He, by the grace of God, might taste death for everyone.

For it was fitting for Him, for whom are all things and by whom are all things, in bringing many sons to glory, to make the captain of their salvation perfect through sufferings.

HEBREWS 2:9–10

Though He was a Son, yet He learned obedience by the things which He suffered.

And having been perfected, He became the author of eternal salvation to all who obey Him.

HEBREWS 5:8–9

If children, then heirs—heirs of God and joint heirs with Christ, if indeed we suffer with Him, that we may also be glorified together.

For I consider that the sufferings of this present time are not worthy to be compared with the glory which shall be revealed in us.

ROMANS 8:17–18

The love of money is a root of all kinds of evil, for which some have strayed from the faith in their greediness, and pierced themselves through with many sorrows.

But you, O man of God, flee these things and pursue righteousness, godliness, faith, love, patience, gentleness.

1 TIMOTHY 6:10–11

Not that I speak in regard to need, for I have learned in whatever state I am, to be content: I know how to be abased, and I know how to abound. Everywhere and in all things I have learned both to be full and to be hungry, both to abound and to suffer need.

I can do all things through Christ who strengthens me.

PHILIPPIANS 4:11–13

Trust in the LORD, and do good;
Dwell in the land, and feed on His faithfulness.
Delight yourself also in the LORD,
And He shall give you the desires of your heart.

PSALM 37:3–4

Command those who are rich in this present age not to be haughty, nor to trust in uncertain riches but in the living God, who gives us richly all things to enjoy.

Let them do good, that they be rich in good works, ready to give, willing to share, storing up for themselves a good foundation for the time to come, that they may lay hold on eternal life.

1 TIMOTHY 6:17–19

Then He said to His disciples, "Therefore I say to you, do not worry about your life, what you will eat; nor about the body, what you will put on.

"Life is more than food, and the body is more than clothing.

"Consider the ravens, for they neither sow nor reap, which have neither storehouse nor barn; and God feeds them. Of how much more value are you than the birds?"

LUKE 12:22–24

So we may boldly say: "The LORD is my helper; I will not fear. What can man do to me?"

HEBREWS 13:6

My God shall supply all your need according to His riches in glory by Christ Jesus.

PHILIPPIANS 4:19

He who trusts in his riches will fall, but the righteous will flourish like foliage.

PROVERBS 11:28

There is one who makes himself rich, yet has nothing; and one who makes himself poor, yet has great riches.
Wealth gained by dishonesty will be diminished, but he who gathers by labor will increase.

PROVERBS 13:7, 11

Remove falsehood and lies far from me; give me neither poverty nor riches—feed me with the food allotted to me.

PROVERBS 30:8

For you have need of endurance, so that after you have done the will of God, you may receive the promise:

HEBREWS 10:36

Listen, my beloved brethren: Has God not chosen the poor of this world to be rich in faith and heirs of the kingdom which He promised to those who love Him?

JAMES 2:5

Peace I leave with you, My peace I give to you; not as the world gives do I give to you. Let not your heart be troubled, neither let it be afraid.

JOHN 14:27

Be anxious for nothing, but in everything by prayer and supplication, with thanksgiving, let your requests be made known to God; and the peace of God, which surpasses all understanding, will guard your hearts and minds through Christ Jesus.

Finally, brethren, whatever things are true, whatever things are noble, whatever things are just, whatever things are pure, whatever things are lovely, whatever things are of good report, if there is any virtue and if there is anything praiseworthy—meditate on these things.

PHILIPPIANS 4:6–8

Fear not, for I am with you;
Be not dismayed, for I am your God.
I will strengthen you,
Yes, I will help you,
I will uphold you with My righteous right hand.'

ISAIAH 41:10

He makes me to lie down in green pastures;
He leads me beside the still waters.
He restores my soul;
He leads me in the paths of righteousness
For His name's sake.
Yea, though I walk through the valley of the
      shadow of death,
I will fear no evil;
For You are with me;
Your rod and Your staff, they comfort me.

PSALM 23:2–4

Casting all your care upon Him, for He cares for you.

Be sober, be vigilant; because your adversary the devil walks about like a roaring lion, seeking whom he may devour.

Resist him, steadfast in the faith, knowing that the same sufferings are experienced by your brotherhood in the world.

But may the God of all grace, who called us to His eternal glory by Christ Jesus, after you have suffered a while, perfect, establish, strengthen, and settle you.

1 PETER 5:7–10

God is our refuge and strength,
A very present help in trouble.
Therefore we will not fear,
Even though the earth be removed,
And though the mountains be carried into the
      midst of the sea;
Though its waters roar and be troubled,
Though the mountains shake with its
      swelling. Selah

PSALM 46:1–3

"Be angry, and do not sin": do not let the sun go down on your wrath, nor give place to the devil.

EPHESIANS 4:26–27

But He was in the stern, asleep on a pillow. And they awoke Him and said to Him, "Teacher, do You not care that we are perishing?"

Then He arose and rebuked the wind, and said to the sea, "Peace, be still!" And the wind ceased and there was a great calm.

But He said to them, "Why are you so fearful? How is it that you have no faith?"

MARK 4:38–40

Surely He shall deliver you from the snare of
    the fowler
And from the perilous pestilence.
He shall cover you with His feathers,
And under His wings you shall take refuge;
His truth shall be your shield and buckler.
You shall not be afraid of the terror by night,
Nor of the arrow that flies by day,
Nor of the pestilence that walks in darkness,
Nor of the destruction that lays waste at
    noonday.
A thousand may fall at your side,
And ten thousand at your right hand;
But it shall not come near you.

PSALM 91:3–7

Whenever I am afraid,
I will trust in You.
In God (I will praise His word),
In God I have put my trust;
I will not fear.
What can flesh do to me?

PSALM 56:3–4

We are hard pressed on every side, yet not crushed; we are perplexed, but not in despair; persecuted, but not forsaken; struck down, but not destroyed—

Therefore we do not lose heart. Even though our outward man is perishing, yet the inward man is being renewed day by day.

For our light affliction, which is but for a moment, is working for us a far more exceeding and eternal weight of glory, while we do not look at the things which are seen, but at the things which are not seen. For the things which are seen are temporary, but the things which are not seen are eternal.

2 CORINTHIANS 4:8–9, 16–18

Let your conduct be without covetousness; be content with such things as you have. For He Himself has said, "I will never leave you nor forsake you." So we may boldly say: "The LORD is my helper; I will not fear. What can man do to me?"

HEBREWS 13:5–6

Come to Me, all you who labor and are heavy laden, and I will give you rest.

MATTHEW 11:28

For His anger is but for a moment,
His favor is for life;
Weeping may endure for a night,
But joy comes in the morning.
I cried out to You, O LORD;
And to the LORD I made supplication:
"What profit is there in my blood,
When I go down to the pit?
Will the dust praise You?
Will it declare Your truth?
Hear, O LORD, and have mercy on me;
LORD, be my helper!"
You have turned for me my mourning into
     dancing;
You have put off my sackcloth and clothed me
     with gladness,
To the end that my glory may sing praise to
     You and not be silent.
O LORD my God, I will give thanks to You
     forever.

PSALM 30:5, 8–12

This hope we have as an anchor of the soul, both sure
and steadfast, and which enters the Presence behind
the veil.

HEBREWS 6:19

Finally, brethren, whatever things are true, whatever things are noble, whatever things are just, whatever things are pure, whatever things are lovely, whatever things are of good report, if there is any virtue and if there is anything praiseworthy—meditate on these things.

PHILIPPIANS 4:8

> He has not dealt with us according to our
>   sins,
> Nor punished us according to our iniquities.
> For as the heavens are high above the earth,
> So great is His mercy toward those who fear
>   Him;
> As far as the east is from the west,
> So far has He removed our transgressions
>   from us.

PSALM 103:10–12

After he had patiently endured, he obtained the promise.

HEBREWS 6:15

Let us not grow weary while doing good, for in due season we shall reap if we do not lose heart.

GALATIANS 6:9

Through the LORD's mercies we are not con-
sumed,
Because His compassions fail not.
They are new every morning;
Great is Your faithfulness.
"The LORD is my portion," says my soul,
"Therefore I hope in Him!"

LAMENTATIONS 3:22–24

But let us who are of the day be sober, putting on the
breastplate of faith and love, and as a helmet the hope
of salvation.

For God did not appoint us to wrath, but to
obtain salvation through our Lord Jesus Christ.

1 THESSALONIANS 5:8–9

Therefore do not worry about tomorrow, for tomorrow will worry about its own things. Sufficient for the
day is its own trouble.

MATTHEW 6:34

You are my hiding place and my shield; I hope in
Your word.

PSALM 119:114

Behold, the eye of the LORD is on those who
    fear Him,
On those who hope in His mercy,
To deliver their soul from death,
And to keep them alive in famine.
Our soul waits for the LORD;
He is our help and our shield.
For our heart shall rejoice in Him,
Because we have trusted in His holy name.
Let Your mercy, O LORD, be upon us,
Just as we hope in You.

PSALM 33:18–22

Let your conduct be without covetousness; be content with such things as you have. For He Himself
has said, "I will never leave you nor forsake you."

So we may boldly say: "The LORD is my helper;
I will not fear. What can man do to me?"

HEBREWS 13:5–6

Now may the God of hope fill you with all joy and
peace in believing, that you may abound in hope by
the power of the Holy Spirit.

ROMANS 15:13

Cast your burden on the LORD, and He shall sustain
you; He shall never permit the righteous to be moved.

PSALM 55:22

My soul, wait silently for God alone,
For my expectation is from Him.
He only is my rock and my salvation;
He is my defense;
I shall not be moved.
In God is my salvation and my glory;
The rock of my strength,
And my refuge, is in God.

PSALM 62:5–7

Those who wait on the LORD
Shall renew their strength;
They shall mount up with wings like eagles,
They shall run and not be weary,
They shall walk and not faint.

ISAIAH 40:31

Commit your way to the LORD,
Trust also in Him,
And He shall bring it to pass.
He shall bring forth your righteousness as the
 light,
And your justice as the noonday.
Rest in the LORD, and wait patiently for Him;
Do not fret because of him who prospers in
 his way,
Because of the man who brings wicked
 schemes to pass.

PSALM 37:5–7

There remains therefore a rest for the people of God.

Let us therefore be diligent to enter that rest, lest anyone fall according to the same example of disobedience.

Seeing then that we have a great High Priest who has passed through the heavens, Jesus the Son of God, let us hold fast our confession.

HEBREWS 4:9, 11, 14

He said, "My Presence will go with you, and I will give you rest."

EXODUS 33:14

Therefore, having been justified by faith, we have peace with God through our Lord Jesus Christ, through whom also we have access by faith into this grace in which we stand, and rejoice in hope of the glory of God.

ROMANS 5:1–2

We know that all things work together for good to those who love God, to those who are the called according to His purpose.

ROMANS 8:28

God is not the author of confusion but of peace, as in all the churches of the saints.

1 CORINTHIANS 14:33

Cast your burden on the LORD, and He shall sustain you; He shall never permit the righteous to be moved.

PSALM 55:22

The fear of man brings a snare, but whoever trusts in the LORD shall be safe.

PROVERBS 29:25

Blessed is the man who trusts in the LORD,
And whose hope is the LORD.
For he shall be like a tree planted by the waters,
Which spreads out its roots by the river,
And will not fear when heat comes;
But its leaf will be green,
And will not be anxious in the year of drought,
Nor will cease from yielding fruit.

JEREMIAH 17:7–8

We know that all things work together for good to those who love God, to those who are the called according to His purpose.

ROMANS 8:28

He will not be afraid of evil tidings;
His heart is steadfast, trusting in the LORD.
His heart is established;
He will not be afraid,
Until he sees his desire upon his enemies.

PSALM 112:7–8

I will say of the Lord, "He is my refuge and
    my fortress;
My God, in Him I will trust."
Surely He shall deliver you from the snare of
    the fowler
And from the perilous pestilence.
He shall cover you with His feathers,
And under His wings you shall take refuge;
His truth shall be your shield and buckler.

PSALM 91:2–4

Casting all your care upon Him, for He cares for you.

1 PETER 5:7

Yes, we had the sentence of death in ourselves, that
we should not trust in ourselves but in God who
raises the dead, who delivered us from so great a
death, and does deliver us; in whom we trust that He
will still deliver us.

2 CORINTHIANS 1:9–10

Therefore we will not fear, even though the earth be
removed, and though the mountains be carried into
the midst of the sea.

PSALM 46:2

Through God we will do valiantly, for it is He
who shall tread down our enemies.

PSALM 60:12

The LORD is on my side;
I will not fear.
What can man do to me?
It is better to trust in the LORD
Than to put confidence in man.

PSALM 118:6, 8

He will not allow your foot to be moved; He
who keeps you will not slumber.

PSALM 121:3

Those who trust in the LORD
Are like Mount Zion,
Which cannot be moved, but abides forever.
Do good, O LORD, to those who are good,
And to those who are upright in their hearts.

PSALM 125:1, 4

He who heeds the word wisely will find good, and
whoever trusts in the LORD, happy is he.

PROVERBS 16:20

The righteous shall flourish like a palm tree,
He shall grow like a cedar in Lebanon.
Those who are planted in the house of the
    LORD
Shall flourish in the courts of our God.
They shall still bear fruit in old age;
They shall be fresh and flourishing,
To declare that the LORD is upright;
He is my rock, and there is no
    unrighteousness in Him.

PSALM 92:12–15

For by me your days will be multiplied, and years of life will be added to you.

PROVERBS 9:11

Who satisfies your mouth with good things, so that your youth is renewed like the eagle's.

PSALM 103:5

Therefore remove sorrow from your heart, and put away evil from your flesh, for childhood and youth are vanity.

ECCLESIASTES 11:10

God's Answers

The days of our lives are seventy years;
And if by reason of strength they are eighty
        years,
Yet their boast is only labor and sorrow;
For it is soon cut off, and we fly away.
So teach us to number our days,
That we may gain a heart of wisdom.
Oh, satisfy us early with Your mercy,
That we may rejoice and be glad all our days!

PSALM 90:10, 12, 14

None of us lives to himself, and no one dies to himself.
    For if we live, we live to the Lord; and if we die,
we die to the Lord. Therefore, whether we live or die,
we are the Lord's.

ROMANS 14:7–8

For I know that my Redeemer lives,
And He shall stand at last on the earth;
And after my skin is destroyed, this I know,
That in my flesh I shall see God,
Whom I shall see for myself,
And my eyes shall behold, and not another.
How my heart yearns within me!

JOB 19:25–27

That the older men be sober, reverent, temperate, sound in faith, in love, in patience; the older women likewise, that they be reverent in behavior, not slanderers, not given to much wine, teachers of good things—that they admonish the young women to love their husbands, to love their children.

TITUS 2:2–4

For this is God, our God forever and ever;
He will be our guide even to death.

PSALM 48:14

The fear of the LORD prolongs days, but the years of the wicked will be shortened.

PROVERBS 10:27

You shall come to the grave at a full age, as a sheaf of grain ripens in its season.

JOB 5:26

For we know that if our earthly house, this tent, is destroyed, we have a building from God, a house not made with hands, eternal in the heavens.

2 CORINTHIANS 5:1

We do not look at the things which are seen, but at the things which are not seen. For the things which are seen are temporary, but the things which are not seen are eternal.

2 CORINTHIANS 4:18

When you pass through the waters, I will be
    with you;
And through the rivers, they shall not over-
    flow you.
When you walk through the fire, you shall
    not be burned,
Nor shall the flame scorch you.

ISAIAH 43:2

Let all those rejoice who put their trust in
    You;
Let them ever shout for joy, because You
    defend them;
Let those also who love Your name
Be joyful in You.
For You, O LORD, will bless the righteous;
With favor You will surround him as with a
    shield.

PSALM 5:11–12

The angel of the LORD encamps all around those who
fear Him, and delivers them.

PSALM 34:7

He who dwells in the secret place of the Most
      High
Shall abide under the shadow of the Almighty.
I will say of the LORD, "He is my refuge and
      my fortress;
My God, in Him I will trust."
Surely He shall deliver you from the snare of
      the fowler   •
And from the perilous pestilence.
He shall cover you with His feathers,
And under His wings you shall take refuge;
His truth shall be your shield and buckler.
You shall not be afraid of the terror by night,
Nor of the arrow that flies by day,
Nor of the pestilence that walks in darkness,
Nor of the destruction that lays waste at
      noonday.
A thousand may fall at your side,
And ten thousand at your right hand;
But it shall not come near you.
Only with your eyes shall you look,
And see the reward of the wicked.
Because you have made the LORD, who is my
      refuge,
Even the Most High, your dwelling place,
No evil shall befall you,
Nor shall any plague come near your dwelling.

PSALM 91:1–10

The horse is prepared for the day of battle, but deliverance is of the LORD.

PROVERBS 21:31

The fear of man brings a snare, but whoever trusts in the LORD shall be safe.

PROVERBS 29:25

I will both lie down in peace, and sleep; for You alone, O LORD, make me dwell in safety.

PSALM 4:8

Yea, though I walk through the valley of the
        shadow of death,
I will fear no evil;
For You are with me;
Your rod and Your staff, they comfort me.

PSALM 23:4

So shall they fear
The name of the LORD from the west,
And His glory from the rising of the sun;
When the enemy comes in like a flood,
The Spirit of the LORD will lift up a standard
        against him.

ISAIAH 59:19

"Therefore do not worry, saying, 'What shall we eat?' or 'What shall we drink?' or 'What shall we wear?'

"For after all these things the Gentiles seek. For your heavenly Father knows that you need all these things.

"But seek first the kingdom of God and His righteousness, and all these things shall be added to you.

"Therefore do not worry about tomorrow, for tomorrow will worry about its own things. Sufficient for the day is its own trouble."

MATTHEW 6:31–34

You will keep him in perfect peace,
Whose mind is stayed on You,
Because he trusts in You.
Trust in the LORD forever,
For in YAH, the LORD, is everlasting strength.

ISAIAH 26:3–4

Let your conduct be without covetousness; be content with such things as you have. For He Himself has said, "I will never leave you nor forsake you."

So we may boldly say: "The LORD is my helper; I will not fear. What can man do to me?"

HEBREWS 13:5–6

Be anxious for nothing, but in everything by prayer and supplication, with thanksgiving, let your requests be made known to God; and the peace of God, which surpasses all understanding, will guard your hearts and minds through Christ Jesus.

Not that I speak in regard to need, for I have learned in whatever state I am, to be content: I know how to be abased, and I know how to abound. Everywhere and in all things I have learned both to be full and to be hungry, both to abound and to suffer need.

I can do all things through Christ who strengthens me.

PHILIPPIANS 4:6, 7, 11–13

We know that all things work together for good to those who love God, to those who are the called according to His purpose.

ROMANS 8:28

Now godliness with contentment is great gain.

For we brought nothing into this world, and it is certain we can carry nothing out.

And having food and clothing, with these we shall be content.

1 TIMOTHY 6:6–8

He who dwells in the secret place of the Most
  High
Shall abide under the shadow of the Almighty.
I will say of the LORD, "He is my refuge and
  my fortress;
My God, in Him I will trust."

PSALM 91:1–2

But I discipline my body and bring it into subjection,
lest, when I have preached to others, I myself should
become disqualified.

1 CORINTHIANS 9:27

The LORD upholds all who fall,
And raises up all who are bowed down.
The eyes of all look expectantly to You,
And You give them their food in due season.
You open Your hand
And satisfy the desire of every living thing.

PSALM 145:14–16

To be carnally minded is death, but to be spiritually
minded is life and peace.

ROMANS 8:6

MINISTERING IN CHRIST

—— ❧❧ ——

What Is True Service?

When He had called the people to Himself, with His disciples also, He said to them, "Whoever desires to come after Me, let him deny himself, and take up his cross, and follow Me.

"For whoever desires to save his life will lose it, but whoever loses his life for My sake and the gospel's will save it.

"For what will it profit a man if he gains the whole world, and loses his own soul?

"Or what will a man give in exchange for his soul?"

MARK 8:34–37

Abide in Me, and I in you. As the branch cannot bear fruit of itself, unless it abides in the vine, neither can you, unless you abide in Me.

I am the vine, you are the branches. He who abides in Me, and I in him, bears much fruit; for without Me you can do nothing.

JOHN 15:4–5

By this all will know that you are My disciples, if you have love for one another.

JOHN 13:35

He who calls you is faithful, who also will do it.

1 THESSALONIANS 5:24

For we do not preach ourselves, but Christ Jesus the Lord, and ourselves your bondservants for Jesus' sake.

For it is the God who commanded light to shine out of darkness, who has shone in our hearts to give the light of the knowledge of the glory of God in the face of Jesus Christ.

But we have this treasure in earthen vessels, that the excellence of the power may be of God and not of us.

2 CORINTHIANS 4:5–7

And whatever you do, do it heartily, as to the Lord and not to men, knowing that from the Lord you will receive the reward of the inheritance; for you serve the Lord Christ.

But he who does wrong will be repaid for what he has done, and there is no partiality.

COLOSSIANS 3:23–25

So the people asked him, saying, "What shall we do then?"

He answered and said to them, "He who has two tunics, let him give to him who has none; and he who has food, let him do likewise."

LUKE 3:10–11

You did not choose Me, but I chose you and appointed you that you should go and bear fruit, and that your fruit should remain, that whatever you ask the Father in My name He may give you.

These things I command you, that you love one another.

JOHN 15:16–17

That you may become blameless and harmless, children of God without fault in the midst of a crooked and perverse generation, among whom you shine as lights in the world, holding fast the word of life, so that I may rejoice in the day of Christ that I have not run in vain or labored in vain.

PHILIPPIANS 2:15–16

Command those who are rich in this present age not to be haughty, nor to trust in uncertain riches but in the living God, who gives us richly all things to enjoy.

Let them do good, that they be rich in good works, ready to give, willing to share, storing up for themselves a good foundation for the time to come, that they may lay hold on eternal life.

1 TIMOTHY 6:17–19

Be anxious for nothing, but in everything by prayer and supplication, with thanksgiving, let your requests be made known to God; and the peace of God, which surpasses all understanding, will guard your hearts and minds through Christ Jesus.

PHILIPPIANS 4:6–7

Assuredly, I say to you, whatever you bind on earth will be bound in heaven, and whatever you loose on earth will be loosed in heaven.

Again I say to you that if two of you agree on earth concerning anything that they ask, it will be done for them by My Father in heaven.

MATTHEW 18:18–19

Let us therefore come boldly to the throne of grace, that we may obtain mercy and find grace to help in time of need.

HEBREWS 4:16

Without faith it is impossible to please Him, for he who comes to God must believe that He is, and that He is a rewarder of those who diligently seek Him.

HEBREWS 11:6

313

Confess your trespasses to one another, and pray for one another, that you may be healed. The effective, fervent prayer of a righteous man avails much.

Elijah was a man with a nature like ours, and he prayed earnestly that it would not rain; and it did not rain on the land for three years and six months.

And he prayed again, and the heaven gave rain, and the earth produced its fruit.

JAMES 5:16–18

Now in the morning, having risen a long while before daylight, He went out and departed to a solitary place; and there He prayed.

MARK 1:35

Now it came to pass in those days that He went out to the mountain to pray, and continued all night in prayer to God.

LUKE 6:12

LORD, I cry out to You;
Make haste to me!
Give ear to my voice when I cry out to You.
Let my prayer be set before You as incense,
The lifting up of my hands as the evening
    sacrifice.

PSALM 141:1–2

So shall My word be that goes forth from My mouth; it shall not return to Me void, but it shall accomplish what I please, and it shall prosper in the thing for which I sent it.

ISAIAH 55:11

So I say to you, ask, and it will be given to you; seek, and you will find; knock, and it will be opened to you.

LUKE 11:9

Then He spoke a parable to them, that men always ought to pray and not lose heart.

LUKE 18:1

For the eyes of the LORD are on the righteous,
And His ears are open to their prayers;
But the face of the LORD is against those who
    do evil.

1 PETER 3:12

Evening and morning and at noon I will pray, and cry aloud, and He shall hear my voice.

PSALM 55:17

When you pray, you shall not be like the hypocrites. For they love to pray standing in the synagogues and on the corners of the streets, that they may be seen by men. Assuredly, I say to you, they have their reward.

But you, when you pray, go into your room, and when you have shut your door, pray to your Father who is in the secret place; and your Father who sees in secret will reward you openly.

MATTHEW 6:5–6

You are the light of the world. A city that is set on a hill cannot be hidden.

Nor do they light a lamp and put it under a basket, but on a lampstand, and it gives light to all who are in the house.

Let your light so shine before men, that they may see your good works and glorify your Father in heaven.

MATTHEW 5:14–16

No one, when he has lit a lamp, puts it in a secret place or under a basket, but on a lampstand, that those who come in may see the light.

LUKE 11:33

Therefore settle it in your hearts not to meditate beforehand on what you will answer; for I will give you a mouth and wisdom which all your adversaries will not be able to contradict or resist.

LUKE 21:14-15

I will sing to the LORD as long as I live;
I will sing praise to my God while I have my being.

PSALM 104:33

But that the world may know that I love the Father, and as the Father gave Me commandment, so I do. Arise, let us go from here.

JOHN 14:31

Praying always with all prayer and supplication in the Spirit, being watchful to this end with all perseverance and supplication for all the saints—and for me, that utterance may be given to me, that I may open my mouth boldly to make known the mystery of the gospel, for which I am an ambassador in chains; that in it I may speak boldly, as I ought to speak.

EPHESIANS 6:18–20

Therefore do not be ashamed of the testimony of our Lord, nor of me His prisoner, but share with me in the sufferings for the gospel according to the power of God, who has saved us and called us with a holy calling, not according to our works, but according to His own purpose and grace which was given to us in Christ Jesus before time began, but has now been revealed by the appearing of our Savior Jesus Christ, who has abolished death and brought life and immortality to light through the gospel.

2 TIMOTHY 1:8–10

Finally, all of you be of one mind, having compassion for one another; love as brothers, be tenderhearted, be courteous; not returning evil for evil or reviling for reviling, but on the contrary blessing, knowing that you were called to this, that you may inherit a blessing.

For "He who would love life and see good days, let him refrain his tongue from evil, and his lips from speaking deceit.

Let him turn away from evil and do good; let him seek peace and pursue it.

But sanctify the Lord God in your hearts, and always be ready to give a defense to

everyone who asks you a reason for the hope that is in you, with meekness and fear.

1 PETER 3:8–11, 15

Also I say to you, whoever confesses Me before men, him the Son of Man also will confess before the angels of God.

But he who denies Me before men will be denied before the angels of God.

LUKE 12:8–9

The fruit of the righteous is a tree of life,
And he who wins souls is wise.

PROVERBS 11:30

Blessed are you when men hate you,
And when they exclude you,
And revile you, and cast out your name as evil,
For the Son of Man's sake.
Rejoice in that day and leap for joy!
For indeed your reward is great in heaven,
For in like manner their fathers did to the
      prophets.

LUKE 6:22–23

If the world hates you, you know that it hated Me before it hated you.

If you were of the world, the world would love its own. Yet because you are not of the world, but I chose you out of the world, therefore the world hates you.

Remember the word that I said to you, "A servant is not greater than his master." If they persecuted Me, they will also persecute you. If they kept My word, they will keep yours also.

But all these things they will do to you for My name's sake, because they do not know Him who sent Me.

JOHN 15:18–21

But even if you should suffer for righteousness' sake, you are blessed. And do not be afraid of their threats, nor be troubled.

But sanctify the Lord God in your hearts, and always be ready to give a defense to everyone who asks you a reason for the hope that is in you, with meekness and fear; having a good conscience, that when they defame you as evildoers, those who revile your good conduct in Christ may be ashamed.

1 PETER 3:14–16

If you are reproached for the name of Christ, blessed are you, for the Spirit of glory and of God rests upon you. On their part He is blasphemed, but on your part He is glorified.

Yet if anyone suffers as a Christian, let him not be ashamed, but let him glorify God in this matter.

1 PETER 4:14, 16

Therefore, having been justified by faith, we have peace with God through our Lord Jesus Christ, through whom also we have access by faith into this grace in which we stand, and rejoice in hope of the glory of God.

ROMANS 5:1–2

The LORD has been my defense,
And my God the rock of my refuge.
He has brought on them their own iniquity,
And shall cut them off in their own wicked-
    ness;
The LORD our God shall cut them off.

PSALM 94:22–23

My eyes shall be on the faithful of the land,
That they may dwell with me;
He who walks in a perfect way,
He shall serve me.
He who works deceit shall not dwell within
    my house;
He who tells lies shall not continue in my
    presence.

PSALM 101:6–7

Persecutions, afflictions, which happened to me at Antioch, at Iconium, at Lystra—what persecutions I endured. And out of them all the Lord delivered me.

Yes, and all who desire to live godly in Christ Jesus will suffer persecution.

2 TIMOTHY 3:11–12

Do not say, "I will recompense evil"; wait for the LORD, and He will save you.

PROVERBS 20:22

The LORD will guide you continually,
And satisfy your soul in drought,
And strengthen your bones;
You shall be like a watered garden,
And like a spring of water, whose waters do
    not fail.

ISAIAH 58:11

I say to you that likewise there will be more joy in heaven over one sinner who repents than over ninety-nine just persons who need no repentance.

LUKE 15:7

"For My thoughts are not your thoughts,
Nor are your ways My ways," says the LORD.
"For as the heavens are higher than the earth,
So are My ways higher than your ways,
And My thoughts than your thoughts."

ISAIAH 55:8–9

Beloved, do not believe every spirit, but test the spirits, whether they are of God; because many false prophets have gone out into the world.

1 JOHN 4:1

The Lord is not slack concerning His promise, as some count slackness, but is longsuffering toward us, not willing that any should perish but that all should come to repentance.

2 PETER 3:9

The Son of Man has come to save that which was lost.

MATTHEW 18:11

The spirit of a man is the lamp of the LORD, searching all the inner depths of his heart.

PROVERBS 20:27

> He found him in a desert land
> And in the wasteland, a howling wilderness;
> He encircled him, He instructed him,
> He kept him as the apple of His eye.
> As an eagle stirs up its nest,
> Hovers over its young,
> Spreading out its wings, taking them up,
> Carrying them on its wings,
> So the LORD alone led him,
> And there was no foreign god with him.

DEUTERONOMY 32:10–12

So he shepherded them according to the integrity of his heart, and guided them by the skillfulness of his hands.

PSALM 78:72

You shall not go out with haste,
Nor go by flight;
For the LORD will go before you,
And the God of Israel will be your rear guard.

ISAIAH 52:12

There are three that bear witness in heaven: the Father, the Word, and the Holy Spirit; and these three are one.

1 JOHN 5:7

A man's heart plans his way,
But the LORD directs his steps.
The lot is cast into the lap,
But its every decision is from the LORD.

PROVERBS 16:9, 33

God has not given us a spirit of fear, but of power and of love and of a sound mind.

2 TIMOTHY 1:7

Rest in the LORD, and wait patiently for Him;
Do not fret because of him who prospers in
    his way,
Because of the man who brings wicked
    schemes to pass.
Cease from anger, and forsake wrath;
Do not fret—it only causes harm.
For evildoers shall be cut off;
But those who wait on the LORD,
They shall inherit the earth.

PSALM 37:7–9

I waited patiently for the LORD;
And He inclined to me,
And heard my cry.
He also brought me up out of a horrible pit,
Out of the miry clay,
And set my feet upon a rock,
And established my steps.
He has put a new song in my mouth—
Praise to our God;
Many will see it and fear,
And will trust in the LORD.

PSALM 40:1–3

The LORD will wait, that He may be gracious to you; and therefore He will be exalted, that He may have mercy on you. For the LORD is a God of justice; blessed are all those who wait for Him.

ISAIAH 30:18

Indeed, let no one who waits on You be
    ashamed;
Let those be ashamed who deal treacherously
    without cause.
Show me Your ways, O LORD;
Teach me Your paths.
Lead me in Your truth and teach me,
For You are the God of my salvation;
On You I wait all the day.
Let integrity and uprightness preserve me,
For I wait for You.

PSALM 25:3–5, 21

Wait on the LORD; be of good courage, and He shall strengthen your heart; wait, I say, on the LORD!

PSALM 27:14

I will look to the LORD; I will wait for the God of my salvation; my God will hear me.

MICAH 7:7

Those who wait on the LORD
Shall renew their strength;
They shall mount up with wings like eagles,
They shall run and not be weary,
They shall walk and not faint.

ISAIAH 40:31

The LORD is good to those who wait for Him,
To the soul who seeks Him.
It is good that one should hope and wait quietly
For the salvation of the LORD.

LAMENTATIONS 3:25–26

My soul, wait silently for God alone,
For my expectation is from Him.
He only is my rock and my salvation;
He is my defense;
I shall not be moved.

PSALM 62:5–6

And it will be said in that day:
"Behold, this is our God;
We have waited for Him, and He will save us.
This is the LORD;
We have waited for Him;
We will be glad and rejoice in His salvation."

ISAIAH 25:9

Let us hold fast the confession of our hope without wavering, for He who promised is faithful.

HEBREWS 10:23

That all the peoples of the earth may know that the LORD is God; there is no other.

Let your heart therefore be loyal to the LORD our God, to walk in His statutes and keep His commandments, as at this day.

1 KINGS 8:60–61

Be doers of the word, and not hearers only, deceiving yourselves.

JAMES 1:22

Now therefore, if you will indeed obey My voice and keep My covenant, then you shall be a special treasure to Me above all people; for all the earth is Mine.

EXODUS 19:5

Do not be deceived, God is not mocked; for whatever a man sows, that he will also reap.

For he who sows to his flesh will of the flesh reap corruption, but he who sows to the Spirit will of the Spirit reap everlasting life.

GALATIANS 6:7–8

If you love Me, keep My commandments.

JOHN 14:15

But Peter and the other apostles answered and said: "We ought to obey God rather than men."

ACTS 5:29

I discipline my body and bring it into subjection, lest, when I have preached to others, I myself should become disqualified.

1 CORINTHIANS 9:27

Casting down arguments and every high thing that exalts itself against the knowledge of God, bringing every thought into captivity to the obedience of Christ.

2 CORINTHIANS 10:5

Whoever has no rule over his own spirit is like a city broken down, without walls.

PROVERBS 25:28

He who is faithful in what is least is faithful also in much; and he who is unjust in what is least is unjust also in much.

LUKE 16:10

Behold, You desire truth in the inward parts, and in the hidden part You will make me to know wisdom.

PSALM 51:6

The world is passing away, and the lust of it; but he who does the will of God abides forever.

1 JOHN 2:17

If anyone does not abide in Me, he is cast out as a branch and is withered; and they gather them and throw them into the fire, and they are burned.

If you abide in Me, and My words abide in you, you will ask what you desire, and it shall be done for you.

If you keep My commandments, you will abide in My love, just as I have kept My Father's commandments and abide in His love.

JOHN 15:6–7, 10

Now the just shall live by faith; but if anyone draws back, My soul has no pleasure in him.

HEBREWS 10:38

Then Samuel said:
Has the LORD as great delight in burnt offer-
    ings and sacrifices,
As in obeying the voice of the LORD?
Behold, to obey is better than sacrifice,
And to heed than the fat of rams.

1 SAMUEL 15:22

GIVING TO GOD'S WORK

Do not lay up for yourselves treasures on earth, where moth and rust destroy and where thieves break in and steal; but lay up for yourselves treasures in heaven, where neither moth nor rust destroys and where thieves do not break in and steal.

For where your treasure is, there your heart will be also.

MATTHEW 6:19–21

Now Jesus sat opposite the treasury and saw how the people put money into the treasury. And many who were rich put in much.

Then one poor widow came and threw in two mites, which make a quadrans.

So He called His disciples to Himself and said to them, "Assuredly, I say to you that this poor widow has put in more than all those who have given to the treasury; for they all put in out of their abundance, but she out of her poverty put in all that she had, her whole livelihood."

MARK 12:41–44

Give to the LORD the glory due His name; bring an offering, and come into His courts.

PSALM 96:8

But this I say: He who sows sparingly will also reap sparingly, and he who sows bountifully will also reap bountifully.

So let each one give as he purposes in his heart, not grudgingly or of necessity; for God loves a cheerful giver.

2 CORINTHIANS 9:6–7

But woe to you Pharisees! For you tithe mint and rue and all manner of herbs, and pass by justice and the love of God. These you ought to have done, without leaving the others undone.

LUKE 11:42

He who is faithful in what is least is faithful also in much; and he who is unjust in what is least is unjust also in much.

Therefore if you have not been faithful in the unrighteous mammon, who will commit to your trust the true riches?

LUKE 16:10–11

He who has a generous eye will be blessed, for he gives of his bread to the poor.

PROVERBS 22:9

Therefore bear fruits worthy of repentance, and do not think to say to yourselves, "We have Abraham as our father." For I say to you that God is able to raise up children to Abraham from these stones.

MATTHEW 3:8–9

Does he thank that servant because he did the things that were commanded him? I think not.

So likewise you, when you have done all those things which you are commanded, say, "We are unprofitable servants. We have done what was our duty to do."

LUKE 17:9–10

As soon as the commandment was circulated, the children of Israel brought in abundance the firstfruits of grain and wine, oil and honey, and of all the produce of the field; and they brought in abundantly the tithe of everything.

2 CHRONICLES 31:5

HOPING IN CHRIST

That if you confess with your mouth the Lord Jesus and believe in your heart that God has raised Him from the dead, you will be saved.

For with the heart one believes unto righteousness, and with the mouth confession is made unto salvation.

For the Scripture says, "Whoever believes on Him will not be put to shame."

For there is no distinction between Jew and Greek, for the same Lord over all is rich to all who call upon Him.

For "whoever calls on the name of the LORD shall be saved."

ROMANS 10:9–13

Seek the LORD while He may be found,
Call upon Him while He is near.
Let the wicked forsake his way,
And the unrighteous man his thoughts;
Let him return to the LORD,
And He will have mercy on him;
And to our God,
For He will abundantly pardon.

ISAIAH 55:6–7

Behold, I stand at the door and knock. If anyone hears My voice and opens the door, I will come in to him and dine with him, and he with Me.

REVELATION 3:20

All that the Father gives Me will come to Me, and the one who comes to Me I will by no means cast out.

And this is the will of Him who sent Me, that everyone who sees the Son and believes in Him may have everlasting life; and I will raise him up at the last day.

No one can come to Me unless the Father who sent Me draws him; and I will raise him up at the last day.

It is written in the prophets, "And they shall all be taught by God." Therefore everyone who has heard and learned from the Father comes to Me.

Not that anyone has seen the Father, except He who is from God; He has seen the Father.

Most assuredly, I say to you, he who believes in Me has everlasting life.

JOHN 6:37, 40, 44–47

Without faith it is impossible to please Him, for he who comes to God must believe that He is, and that He is a rewarder of those who diligently seek Him.

HEBREWS 11:6

The Lord is not slack concerning His promise, as some count slackness, but is longsuffering toward us, not willing that any should perish but that all should come to repentance.

But grow in the grace and knowledge of our Lord and Savior Jesus Christ. To Him be the glory both now and forever. Amen.

2 PETER 3:9, 18

Having been set free from sin, and having become slaves of God, you have your fruit to holiness, and the end, everlasting life.

For the wages of sin is death, but the gift of God is eternal life in Christ Jesus our Lord.

ROMANS 6:22–23

Come now, you who say, "Today or tomorrow we will go to such and such a city, spend a year there, buy and sell, and make a profit"; whereas you do not know what will happen tomorrow. For what is your life? It is even a vapor that appears for a little time and then vanishes away.

Instead you ought to say, "If the Lord wills, we shall live and do this or that."

JAMES 4:13–15

Draw near to God and He will draw near to you. Cleanse your hands, you sinners; and purify your hearts, you double-minded.

Lament and mourn and weep! Let your laughter be turned to mourning and your joy to gloom.

Humble yourselves in the sight of the Lord, and He will lift you up.

JAMES 4:8–10

I love those who love me, and those who seek me diligently will find me.

PROVERBS 8:17

Seek the LORD and His strength;
Seek His face evermore!
Remember His marvelous works which He
　　has done,
His wonders, and the judgments of His
　　mouth,

1 CHRONICLES 16:11–12

In the day when I cried out, You answered me, and made me bold with strength in my soul.

PSALM 138:3

Then you will call upon Me and go and pray to Me, and I will listen to you.

And you will seek Me and find Me, when you search for Me with all your heart.

JEREMIAH 29:12–13

As the deer pants for the water brooks,
So pants my soul for You, O God.
My soul thirsts for God, for the living God.
When shall I come and appear before God?
Deep calls unto deep at the noise of Your
    waterfalls;
All Your waves and billows have gone over me.
The LORD will command His lovingkindness
    in the daytime,
And in the night His song shall be with me—
A prayer to the God of my life.

PSALM 42:1–2, 7–8

In my distress I called upon the LORD, and cried out to my God; He heard my voice from His temple, and my cry came before Him, even to His ears.

PSALM 18:6

The LORD is near to all who call upon Him, to all who call upon Him in truth.

PSALM 145:18

Hear my cry, O God;
Attend to my prayer.
From the end of the earth I will cry to You,
When my heart is overwhelmed;
Lead me to the rock that is higher than I.

PSALM 61:1–2

My soul, wait silently for God alone, for my expectation is from Him.

PSALM 62:5

All that the Father gives Me will come to Me, and the one who comes to Me I will by no means cast out.

JOHN 6:37

And the Spirit and the bride say, "Come!" And let him who hears say, "Come!" And let him who thirsts come. Whoever desires, let him take the water of life freely.

REVELATION 22:17

Have you not known?
Have you not heard?
The everlasting God, the LORD,
The Creator of the ends of the earth,
Neither faints nor is weary.
His understanding is unsearchable.
He gives power to the weak,
And to those who have no might He increases
    strength.
But those who wait on the LORD
Shall renew their strength;
They shall mount up with wings like eagles,
They shall run and not be weary,
They shall walk and not faint.

ISAIAH 40:28–29, 31

For You, Lord, are good, and ready to forgive,
And abundant in mercy to all those who call
    upon You.
Give ear, O LORD, to my prayer;
And attend to the voice of my supplications.
In the day of my trouble I will call upon You,
For You will answer me.

PSALM 86:5–7

I will heal their backsliding, I will love them freely, for My anger has turned away from him.

HOSEA 14:4

"I will seek what was lost and bring back what was driven away, bind up the broken and strengthen what was sick; but I will destroy the fat and the strong, and feed them in judgment.

"Thus they shall know that I, the LORD their God, am with them, and they, the house of Israel, are My people," says the Lord GOD. "You are My flock, the flock of My pasture; you are men, and I am your God."

EZEKIEL 34:16, 30–31

He who covers his sins will not prosper, but whoever confesses and forsakes them will have mercy.

PROVERBS 28:13

> Before I was afflicted I went astray,
> But now I keep Your word.
> You are good, and do good;
> Teach me Your statutes.

PSALM 119:67–68

Poverty and shame will come to him who disdains correction, but he who regards a rebuke will be honored.

PROVERBS 13:18

Now no chastening seems to be joyful for the present, but painful; nevertheless, afterward it yields the peaceable fruit of righteousness to those who have been trained by it.

Therefore strengthen the hands which hang down, and the feeble knees, and make straight paths for your feet, so that what is lame may not be dislocated, but rather be healed.

Pursue peace with all people, and holiness, without which no one will see the Lord.

HEBREWS 12:11–14

Blessed is the man whom You instruct, O
    LORD,
And teach out of Your law,
That You may give him rest from the days of
    adversity,
Until the pit is dug for the wicked.
For the LORD will not cast off His people,
Nor will He forsake His inheritance.

PSALM 94:12–14

When my soul fainted within me,
I remembered the LORD;
And my prayer went up to You,
Into Your holy temple.

JONAH 2:7

By which have been given to us exceedingly great and precious promises, that through these you may be partakers of the divine nature, having escaped the corruption that is in the world through lust.

But also for this very reason, giving all diligence, add to your faith virtue, to virtue knowledge, to knowledge self-control, to self-control perseverance, to perseverance godliness, to godliness brotherly kindness, and to brotherly kindness love.

For if these things are yours and abound, you will be neither barren nor unfruitful in the knowledge of our Lord Jesus Christ.

2 Peter 1:4–8

Let us hold fast the confession of our hope without wavering, for He who promised is faithful.

Therefore do not cast away your confidence, which has great reward.

For you have need of endurance, so that after you have done the will of God, you may receive the promise: For yet a little while, and He who is coming will come and will not tarry.

Hebrews 10:23, 35–37

If you carefully keep all these commandments which I command you to do—to love the LORD your God, to walk in all His ways, and to hold fast to Him—then the LORD will drive out all these nations from before you, and you will dispossess greater and mightier nations than yourselves.

DEUTERONOMY 11:22–23

Only be strong and very courageous, that you may observe to do according to all the law which Moses My servant commanded you; do not turn from it to the right hand or to the left, that you may prosper wherever you go.

JOSHUA 1:7

For assuredly, I say to you, whoever says to this mountain, "Be removed and be cast into the sea," and does not doubt in his heart, but believes that those things he says will be done, he will have whatever he says.

MARK 11:23

Do not become sluggish, but imitate those who through faith and patience inherit the promises.

HEBREWS 6:12

Now faith is the substance of things hoped for, the evidence of things not seen.

But without faith it is impossible to please Him, for he who comes to God must believe that He is, and that He is a rewarder of those who diligently seek Him.

By faith Sarah herself also received strength to conceive seed, and she bore a child when she was past the age, because she judged Him faithful who had promised.

HEBREWS 11:1, 6, 11

Now this is the confidence that we have in Him, that if we ask anything according to His will, He hears us.

And if we know that He hears us, whatever we ask, we know that we have the petitions that we have asked of Him.

1 JOHN 5:14–15

If you are willing and obedient,
You shall eat the good of the land;
But if you refuse and rebel,
You shall be devoured by the sword";
For the mouth of the LORD has spoken.

ISAIAH 1:19–20

If any of you lacks wisdom, let him ask of God, who gives to all liberally and without reproach, and it will be given to him.

But let him ask in faith, with no doubting, for he who doubts is like a wave of the sea driven and tossed by the wind.

For let not that man suppose that he will receive anything from the Lord; he is a double-minded man, unstable in all his ways.

JAMES 1:5–8

For with God nothing will be impossible.

LUKE 1:37

Behold, the LORD's hand is not shortened,
That it cannot save;
Nor His ear heavy,
That it cannot hear.
But your iniquities have separated you from
    your God;
And your sins have hidden His face from you,
So that He will not hear.

ISAIAH 59:1–2

But seek first the kingdom of God and His right-eousness, and all these things shall be added to you.

MATTHEW 6:33

UNDERSTANDING IN CHRIST

※

As for God, His way is perfect;
The word of the LORD is proven;
He is a shield to all who trust in Him.
For who is God, except the LORD?
And who is a rock, except our God?
It is God who arms me with strength,
And makes my way perfect.

PSALM 18:30–32

"For My thoughts are not your thoughts,
Nor are your ways My ways," says the LORD.
"For as the heavens are higher than the earth,
So are My ways higher than your ways,
And My thoughts than your thoughts."

ISAIAH 55:8–9

Jesus said to them, "Have you never read in
        the Scriptures:
"The stone which the builders rejected
Has become the chief cornerstone.
This was the LORD's doing,
And it is marvelous in our eyes"?

MATTHEW 21:42

Though the LORD is on high,
Yet He regards the lowly;
But the proud He knows from afar.
Though I walk in the midst of trouble, You
    will revive me;
You will stretch out Your hand
Against the wrath of my enemies,
And Your right hand will save me.

PSALM 138:6–7

He has made the earth by His power,
He has established the world by His wisdom,
And has stretched out the heavens at His
    discretion.

JEREMIAH 10:12

The LORD is in His holy temple,
The LORD's throne is in heaven;
His eyes behold,
His eyelids test the sons of men.
The LORD tests the righteous,
But the wicked and the one who loves vio-
    lence His soul hates.
For the LORD is righteous,
He loves righteousness;
His countenance beholds the upright.

PSALM 11:4–5, 7

I, the LORD, search the heart,
I test the mind,
Even to give every man according to his ways,
According to the fruit of his doings.

JEREMIAH 17:10

Now therefore, let the fear of the LORD be upon you; take care and do it, for there is no iniquity with the LORD our God, no partiality, nor taking of bribes.

2 CHRONICLES 19:7

As a father pities his children,
So the LORD pities those who fear Him.
For He knows our frame;
He remembers that we are dust.

PSALM 103:13–14

If you then, being evil, know how to give good gifts to your children, how much more will your Father who is in heaven give good things to those who ask Him!

MATTHEW 7:11

Every good gift and every perfect gift is from above, and comes down from the Father of lights, with whom there is no variation or shadow of turning.

JAMES 1:17

The fear of the LORD is the beginning of wisdom; a good understanding have all those who do His commandments. His praise endures forever.

PSALM 111:10

Counsel is mine, and sound wisdom; I am understanding, I have strength.

PROVERBS 8:14

Forsake foolishness and live, and go in the way of understanding. "The fear of the LORD is the beginning of wisdom, and the knowledge of the Holy One is understanding.

PROVERBS 9:6, 10

How much better to get wisdom than gold! And to get understanding is to be chosen rather than silver. The highway of the upright is to depart from evil; he who keeps his way preserves his soul.

PROVERBS 16:16–17

Understanding is a wellspring of life to him who has it. But the correction of fools is folly.

PROVERBS 16:22

Yes, if you cry out for discernment,
And lift up your voice for understanding,
If you seek her as silver,
And search for her as for hidden treasures;
Then you will understand the fear of the
     LORD,
And find the knowledge of God.
For the LORD gives wisdom;
From His mouth come knowledge and under-
     standing;
He stores up sound wisdom for the upright;
He is a shield to those who walk uprightly;
He guards the paths of justice,
And preserves the way of His saints.
Then you will understand righteousness and
     justice,
Equity and every good path.
When wisdom enters your heart,
And knowledge is pleasant to your soul,
Discretion will preserve you;
Understanding will keep you,

PROVERBS 2:3–11

If any of you lacks wisdom, let him ask of God, who
gives to all liberally and without reproach, and it will
be given to him.

JAMES 1:5

Incline your ear, and come to Me.
Hear, and your soul shall live;
And I will make an everlasting covenant
      with you—
The sure mercies of David.
Seek the LORD while He may be found,
Call upon Him while He is near.
"For My thoughts are not your thoughts,
Nor are your ways My ways," says the LORD.
"For as the heavens are higher than the earth,
So are My ways higher than your ways,
And My thoughts than your thoughts.

ISAIAH 55:3, 6, 8–9

But there is a spirit in man, and the breath of the Almighty gives him understanding.

JOB 32:8

The LORD is righteous in all His ways,
Gracious in all His works.
The LORD is near to all who call upon Him,
To all who call upon Him in truth.
He will fulfill the desire of those who fear Him;
He also will hear their cry and save them.

PSALM 145:17–19

He does not delight in the strength of the horse;
He takes no pleasure in the legs of a man.
The LORD takes pleasure in those who fear
    Him,
In those who hope in His mercy.

PSALM 147:10–11

If you seek her as silver,
And search for her as for hidden treasures;
Then you will understand the fear of the LORD,
And find the knowledge of God.

PROVERBS 2:4–5

The fear of the LORD is the beginning of wisdom, and
the knowledge of the Holy One is understanding.

PROVERBS 9:10

The fear of the LORD is the instruction of wisdom, and before honor is humility.

PROVERBS 15:33

The fear of the LORD is the beginning of knowledge, but fools despise wisdom and instruction.

PROVERBS 1:7

In the fear of the LORD there is strong
confidence,
And His children will have a place of refuge.
The fear of the LORD is a fountain of life,
To turn one away from the snares of death.

PROVERBS 14:26-27

The fear of the LORD leads to life, and he who has it will abide in satisfaction; he will not be visited with evil.

PROVERBS 19:23

And to man He said, "Behold, the fear of the Lord, that is wisdom, and to depart from evil is understanding."

JOB 28:28

The fear of the LORD prolongs days, but the years of the wicked will be shortened.

PROVERBS 10:27

Oh, fear the LORD, you His saints! There is no want to those who fear Him.

PSALM 34:9

Praise the LORD! Blessed is the man who fears the LORD, who delights greatly in His commandments.

PSALM 112:1

Let us hear the conclusion of the whole matter:
Fear God and keep His commandments,
For this is man's all.
For God will bring every work into judgment,
Including every secret thing,
Whether good or evil.

ECCLESIASTES 12:13–14

All nations before Him are as nothing,
And they are counted by Him less than
      nothing and worthless.
To whom then will you liken God?
Or what likeness will you compare to Him?
"To whom then will you liken Me,
Or to whom shall I be equal?" says the Holy
      One.
Lift up your eyes on high,
And see who has created these things,
Who brings out their host by number;
He calls them all by name,
By the greatness of His might
And the strength of His power;
Not one is missing.
Have you not known?
Have you not heard?
The everlasting God, the LORD,
The Creator of the ends of the earth,
Neither faints nor is weary.
His understanding is unsearchable.

          ISAIAH 40:17, 18, 25, 26, 28

Great is the LORD, and greatly to be praised;
And His greatness is unsearchable.
One generation shall praise Your works to
    another,
And shall declare Your mighty acts.
Your kingdom is an everlasting kingdom,
And Your dominion endures throughout all
    generations.

PSALM 145:3–4, 13

The LORD is our Judge, the LORD is our Lawgiver, the
LORD is our King; He will save us.

ISAIAH 33:22

Behold, I am the LORD, the God of all flesh. Is there
anything too hard for Me?

JEREMIAH 32:27

The heavens declare the glory of God; and the firmament shows His handiwork.

PSALM 19:1

Whom have I in heaven but You? And there is none upon earth that I desire besides You.

PSALM 73:25

Thus says the LORD:
"Heaven is My throne,
And earth is My footstool.
Where is the house that you will build Me?
And where is the place of My rest?
For all those things My hand has made,
And all those things exist,"
Says the LORD.
"But on this one will I look:
On him who is poor and of a contrite spirit,
And who trembles at My word."

ISAIAH 66:1–2

"Am I a God near at hand," says the LORD,
"And not a God afar off?
Can anyone hide himself in secret places,
So I shall not see him?" says the LORD;
"Do I not fill heaven and earth?" says the LORD.

JEREMIAH 23:23–24

"Where were you when I laid the foundations of the earth?

> Tell Me, if you have understanding.
> Who determined its measurements?
> Surely you know!
> Or who stretched the line upon it?
> To what were its foundations fastened?
> Or who laid its cornerstone,
> When the morning stars sang together,
> And all the sons of God shouted for joy?

JOB 38:4–7

And I heard a loud voice from heaven saying, "Behold, the tabernacle of God is with men, and He will dwell with them, and they shall be His people. God Himself will be with them and be their God.

"And God will wipe away every tear from their eyes; there shall be no more death, nor sorrow, nor crying. There shall be no more pain, for the former things have passed away."

Then He who sat on the throne said, "Behold, I make all things new." And He said to me, "Write, for these words are true and faithful."

And He said to me, "It is done! I am the Alpha and the Omega, the Beginning and the End. I will give of the fountain of the water of life freely to him who thirsts.

REVELATION 21:3–6

And when I saw Him, I fell at His feet as dead. But He laid His right hand on me, saying to me, "Do not be afraid; I am the First and the Last.

"I am He who lives, and was dead, and behold, I am alive forevermore. Amen. And I have the keys of Hades and of Death."

REVELATION 1:17–18

Assuredly, I say to you, I will no longer drink of the fruit of the vine until that day when I drink it new in the kingdom of God.

Mark 14:25

But as it is written: "Eye has not seen, nor ear heard, nor have entered into the heart of man the things which God has prepared for those who love Him."

But God has revealed them to us through His Spirit. For the Spirit searches all things, yes, the deep things of God.

For what man knows the things of a man except the spirit of the man which is in him? Even so no one knows the things of God except the Spirit of God.

1 Corinthians 2:9–11

Those who are wise shall shine
Like the brightness of the firmament,
And those who turn many to righteousness
Like the stars forever and ever.

Daniel 12:3

Surely goodness and mercy shall follow me all the days of my life; and I will dwell in the house of the Lord forever.

Psalm 23:6

Violence shall no longer be heard in your land,
Neither wasting nor destruction within your
    borders;
But you shall call your walls Salvation,
And your gates Praise.
The sun shall no longer be your light by day,
Nor for brightness shall the moon give light
    to you;
But the LORD will be to you an everlasting
    light,
And your God your glory.
Your sun shall no longer go down,
Nor shall your moon withdraw itself;
For the LORD will be your everlasting light,
And the days of your mourning shall be ended.

ISAIAH 60:18–20

For since the beginning of the world
Men have not heard nor perceived by the ear,
Nor has the eye seen any God besides You,
Who acts for the one who waits for Him.

ISAIAH 64:4

For now we see in a mirror, dimly, but then face to
face. Now I know in part, but then I shall know just
as I also am known.

1 CORINTHIANS 13:12

UNITING IN CHRIST

—— ❧❧ ——

For you are still carnal. For where there are envy, strife, and divisions among you, are you not carnal and behaving like mere men?

For when one says, "I am of Paul," and another, "I am of Apollos," are you not carnal?

Who then is Paul, and who is Apollos, but ministers through whom you believed, as the Lord gave to each one?

I planted, Apollos watered, but God gave the increase.

So then neither he who plants is anything, nor he who waters, but God who gives the increase.

Now he who plants and he who waters are one, and each one will receive his own reward according to his own labor.

For we are God's fellow workers; you are God's field, you are God's building.

1 CORINTHIANS 3:3–9

But now God has set the members, each one of them, in the body just as He pleased.

And if they were all one member, where would the body be?

But now indeed there are many members, yet one body.

And the eye cannot say to the hand, "I have no need of you"; nor again the head to the feet, "I have no need of you."

No, much rather, those members of the body which seem to be weaker are necessary.

And those members of the body which we think to be less honorable, on these we bestow greater honor; and our unpresentable parts have greater modesty, but our presentable parts have no need. But God composed the body, having given greater honor to that part which lacks it, that there should be no schism in the body, but that the members should have the same care for one another.

And if one member suffers, all the members suffer with it; or if one member is honored, all the members rejoice with it.

Now you are the body of Christ, and members individually.

1 CORINTHIANS 12:18–27

Now, therefore, you are no longer strangers and foreigners, but fellow citizens with the saints and members of the household of God, having been built on the foundation of the apostles and prophets, Jesus Christ Himself being the chief cornerstone, in whom the whole building, being joined together, grows into a holy temple in the Lord, in whom you also are being built together for a dwelling place of God in the Spirit.

EPHESIANS 2:19–22

Finally, all of you be of one mind, having compassion for one another; love as brothers, be tenderhearted, be courteous; not returning evil for evil or reviling for reviling, but on the contrary blessing, knowing that you were called to this, that you may inherit a blessing.

1 PETER 3:8–9

For where two or three are gathered together in My name, I am there in the midst of them."

Then Peter came to Him and said, "Lord, how often shall my brother sin against me, and I forgive him? Up to seven times?"

Jesus said to him, "I do not say to you, up to seven times, but up to seventy times seven.

MATTHEW 18:20–22

You call me Teacher and Lord, and you say well, for so I am.

If I then, your Lord and Teacher, have washed your feet, you also ought to wash one another's feet.

For I have given you an example, that you should do as I have done to you.

Most assuredly, I say to you, a servant is not greater than his master; nor is he who is sent greater than he who sent him.

If you know these things, blessed are you if you do them.

JOHN 13:13–17

The Lord is not slack concerning His promise, as some count slackness, but is longsuffering toward us, not willing that any should perish but that all should come to repentance.

2 PETER 3:9

> Arise, shine;
> For your light has come!
> And the glory of the LORD is risen upon you.
> For behold, the darkness shall cover the earth,
> And deep darkness the people;
> But the LORD will arise over you,
> And His glory will be seen upon you.

ISAIAH 60:1–2

Therefore be patient, brethren, until the coming of the Lord. See how the farmer waits for the precious fruit of the earth, waiting patiently for it until it receives the early and latter rain.

JAMES 5:7

The earth will be filled with the knowledge of the glory of the LORD, as the waters cover the sea.

HABAKKUK 2:14

And they shall rebuild the old ruins,
They shall raise up the former desolations,
And they shall repair the ruined cities,
The desolations of many generations.
For as the earth brings forth its bud,
As the garden causes the things that are sown
      in it to spring forth,
So the Lord GOD will cause righteousness and
      praise to spring forth before all the
      nations.

ISAIAH 61:4, 11

All the ends of the world
Shall remember and turn to the LORD,
And all the families of the nations
Shall worship before You.
For the kingdom is the LORD's,
And He rules over the nations.

PSALM 22:27–28

This gospel of the kingdom will be preached in all the
world as a witness to all the nations, and then the end
will come.

MATTHEW 24:14

And it shall come to pass afterward
That I will pour out My Spirit on all flesh;
Your sons and your daughters shall prophesy,
Your old men shall dream dreams,
Your young men shall see visions.
And also on My menservants and on My
      maidservants
I will pour out My Spirit in those days.
And I will show wonders in the heavens and
      in the earth:
Blood and fire and pillars of smoke.
The sun shall be turned into darkness,
And the moon into blood,
Before the coming of the great and awesome
      day of the LORD.
And it shall come to pass
That whoever calls on the name of the LORD
Shall be saved.
For in Mount Zion and in Jerusalem there
      shall be deliverance,
As the LORD has said,
Among the remnant whom the LORD calls.

JOEL 2:28–32

Behold, I will do a new thing, now it shall spring forth; shall you not know it? I will even make a road in the wilderness and rivers in the desert.

ISAIAH 43:19

But know this, that in the last days perilous times will come: For men will be lovers of themselves, lovers of money, boasters, proud, blasphemers, disobedient to parents, unthankful, unholy, unloving, unforgiving, slanderers, without self-control, brutal, despisers of good, traitors, headstrong, haughty, lovers of pleasure rather than lovers of God, having a form of godliness but denying its power. And from such people turn away!

2 TIMOTHY 3:1–5

Christ was offered once to bear the sins of many. To those who eagerly wait for Him He will appear a second time, apart from sin, for salvation.

HEBREWS 9:28

And in the latter time of their kingdom, when the transgressors have reached their fullness, a king shall arise, having fierce features, who understands sinister schemes.

DANIEL 8:23

And Jesus answered and said to them: "Take heed that no one deceives you.

"For many will come in My name, saying, 'I am the Christ,' and will deceive many.

"And you will hear of wars and rumors of wars. See that you are not troubled; for all these things must come to pass, but the end is not yet.

"For nation will rise against nation, and kingdom against kingdom. And there will be famines, pestilences, and earthquakes in various places.

"All these are the beginning of sorrows.

"Then they will deliver you up to tribulation and kill you, and you will be hated by all nations for My name's sake.

"And then many will be offended, will betray one another, and will hate one another.

"Then many false prophets will rise up and deceive many.

"And because lawlessness will abound, the love of many will grow cold.

"But he who endures to the end shall be saved.

"And this gospel of the kingdom will be preached in all the world as a witness to all the nations, and then the end will come.

MATTHEW 24:4–14

Then two men will be in the field: one will be taken and the other left.

Watch therefore, for you do not know what hour your Lord is coming.

Therefore you also be ready, for the Son of Man is coming at an hour you do not expect.

MATTHEW 24:40, 42, 44

Now the Spirit expressly says that in latter times some will depart from the faith, giving heed to deceiving spirits and doctrines of demons, speaking lies in hypocrisy, having their own conscience seared with a hot iron, forbidding to marry, and commanding to abstain from foods which God created to be received with thanksgiving by those who believe and know the truth.

1 TIMOTHY 4:1–3

But you, beloved, remember the words which were spoken before by the apostles of our Lord Jesus Christ: how they told you that there would be mockers in the last time who would walk according to their own ungodly lusts.

These are sensual persons, who cause divisions, not having the Spirit.

But you, beloved, building yourselves up on your most holy faith, praying in the Holy Spirit, keep yourselves in the love of God, looking for the mercy of our Lord Jesus Christ unto eternal life.

JUDE 17–21

• PRAYER JOURNAL •

• PRAYER JOURNAL •

_____
_____
_____
_____
_____
_____
_____
_____
_____
_____
_____
_____
_____
_____
_____
_____
_____
_____
_____
_____
_____
_____
_____